is this the way the universe works?

77 verses

Gavin Wade
Paul Conneally
and Friends

Accompanying *77 Verses* are images of plants and rocks from the wood in Bronneger, Drenthe, including pines, oaks and hunebeds (prehistoric megalithic funerary monuments).

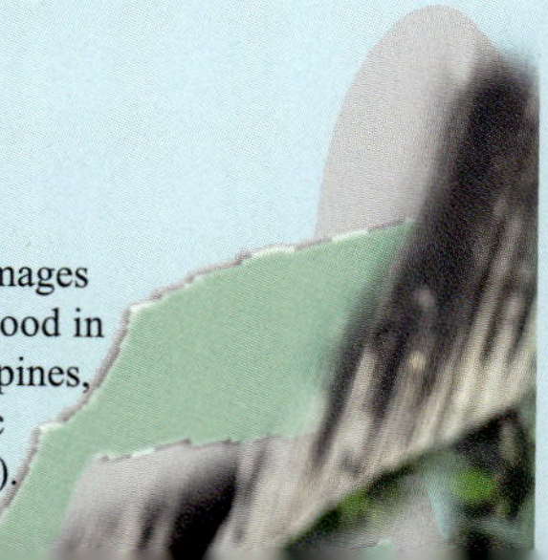

77 Verses
(Is this the way the universe works?)
in het Engels en Nederlands

Gavin Wade and Paul Conneally
and friends

This way around, you can read *77 Verses*.
In the centre of the volume is an interview, *You, Me, and Bashō*, and further information about the authors.

To read *555 Verses* turn the book around.

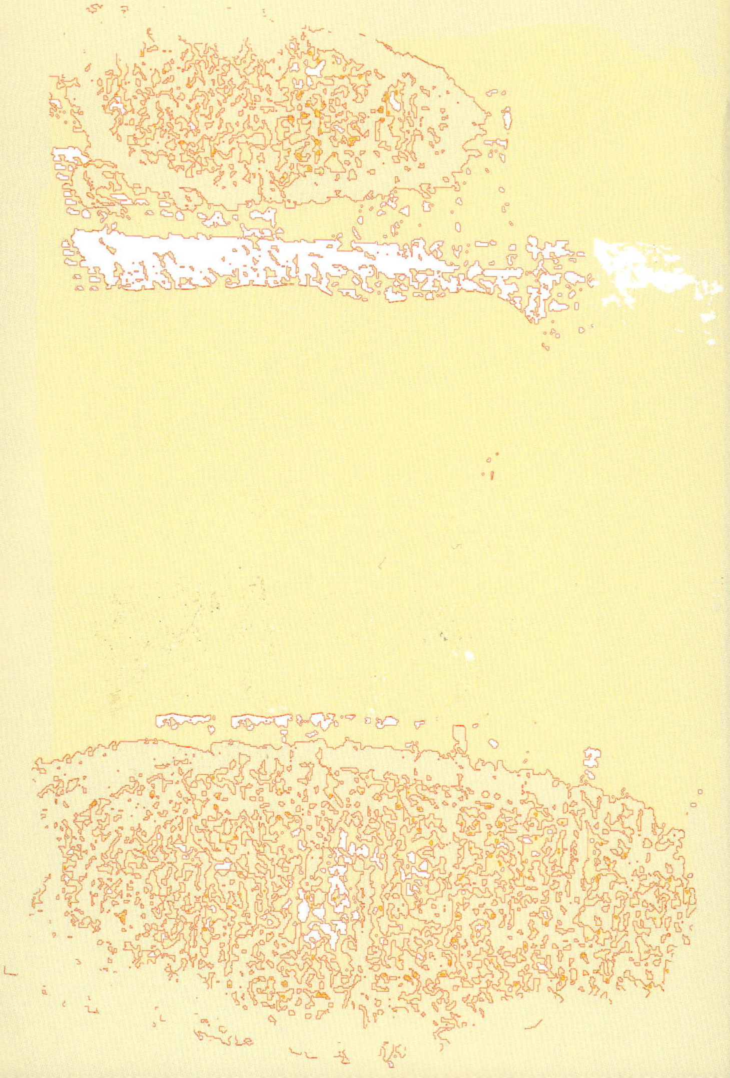

This is a performative book containing performative tanrenga poems to be read out loud. Try reading each verse out loud twice, and listen for the rhythms and cuts. Hear them and connect with the wood, the people that wrote them. Their lives. The past and the present. The future too.

A tanrenga poem looks like a tanka, a five lined Japanese poetry form but it isn't. It's a conversation between a three line haiku like poem and a two line poem written by another writer in response. The two lines can go before or after the three lines. They are connected by the process of link and shift. The two lines linking to the three whilst at the same time shifting away from them. 77 Verses (Is this the way the universe works?) is a collection of such conversations written in and of and out of the woods in Drenthe.

Written from
10.6 – 12.6 2023
with:

Sanne Morssink
M Groenen
Ivo Eise Smit
Renske Marike van Dijk
Sofia Kalotekaris
Hilde de Bruijn

These 77 verses were created collectively during a workshop organised by the Culture & Nature Network and supported by We the North.

This book is published on the occasion of the 4th edition of Into Nature's outdoor biennial, curated by Hilde de Bruijn and Sanne Morssink

'Into Nature: Time Horizons'

Borger-Odoorn, Drenthe, Netherlands
29 July to 29 October 2023

77 Verses (Is this the way the universe works?) is made possible by De Versterking

www.intonature.net

is this the way the universe works?

2023

13.6.23

as I unfold the napkin
Chinese figures
become windmills
a message appearing
in a plate of leftovers

13.6.23

things that remain
reachable, close, secure
language and the wood
the gradual patina
of the sink and bath

13.6.23

hunebed highway
the chaos before
creation
trying to work out which side
of the road the bus goes from

13.6.23

terwijl ik het servet openvouw
worden Chinese figuren
windmolens
een boodschap
op een bord restjes

13.6.23

dingen blijven
bereikbaar, dichtbij, veilig
taal en het hout
het geleidelijke patina
van de wastafel en het bad

13.6.23

hunebed highway
de chaos ur
de schepping
uitvinden aan welke kant
van de weg de bus vertrekt

12.6.23

bird Anselm Kiefer
little shits become
stars in the sky
one constellation
merging into another

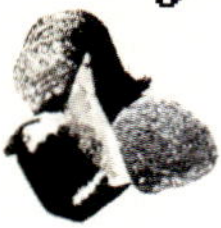

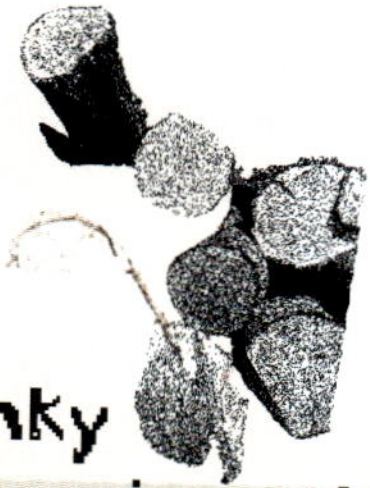

12.6.23

tired and cranky
waiting at the airport
when the two sevens clash
a train whistle blowing
makes a sleepy noise

12.6.23

vogel Anselm Kiefer
kleine poepjes worden
sterren aan de hemel
het ene sterrenbeeld
opgaand in een ander

12.6.23

moe en chagrijnig
wachten op het vliegveld
als de twee zevens botsen
maakt een blazende treinfluit
een slaperig geluid

12.6.23

spiralling wings
the baby birds
waiting to be fed
a gaping hole
in the side of a building

12.6.23

ceremonial poems
appearing lost
twinkles in the light stream
he assures her the dagger
at her neck is just for show

12.6.23

wireworm
the monster in the shadows
of the roots
that's the sound of the men
working on the chain gang

12.6.23

spiraalvormende vleugels
de babyvogels
wachten op hun voer
een gapend gat
in de zijkant van een gebouw

12.6.23

ceremoniële gedichten
lijken verloren
fonkelingen in het licht
hij zegt dat de dolk bij haar nek
slechts voor de show is

12.6.23

draadworm
het monster in de schaduw
van de wortels
dat is het geluid van mannen
die geketend werken

12.6.23

voices in the woods
longing for the night
a possibility
a shin bone
used as a flute

11.6.23

the sun and the wheat
whispering something
in my ear
this time round
the snow won't fall

11.6.23

all the kids like
the burnt out car
splitting the phrase
the swings still swing
in Moscow and Kiev

12.6.23

stemmen in het bos
verlangen naar de nacht
een mogelijkheid
een scheenbeen
gebruikt als een fluit

11.6.23

de zon en het graan
fluisteren iets
in mijn oor
deze rondgang
zal de sneeuw niet vallen

11.6.23

alle kinderen houden van
de uitgebrande auto
zinsplitsing
de schommels schommelen nog
in Moskou en Kiev

11.6.23

under an oak
the woman who grows
my daughter in Spring
whistling and whispering
'I'll do it my way'

11.6.23

setting sail
for new adventures
blocking the light
all the people
rolling through the woods

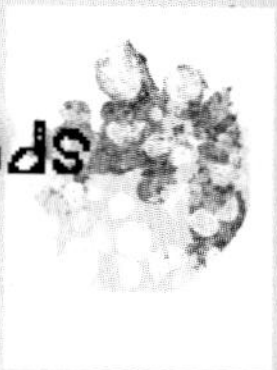

11.6.23

hatching paradox
going into the forest
to write a haiku
a bishop's nest
woven slowly

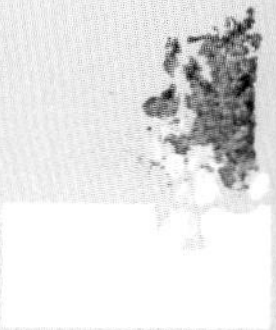

11.6.23

onder een eik
groeit de vrouw
in de lente mijn dochter
fluitend en fluisterend
'I'll do it my way'

11.6.23

het zeil hijsen
voor nieuwe avonturen
het licht blokkeren
alle mensen
rollen door de bossen

11.6.23

broedparadox
het bos ingaan
om een haiku te schrijven
een bisschopsnest
langzaam geweven

11.6.23

bright summer day
under the roof of a tree
piercing leaves
whoever passes by
waves hey hey!

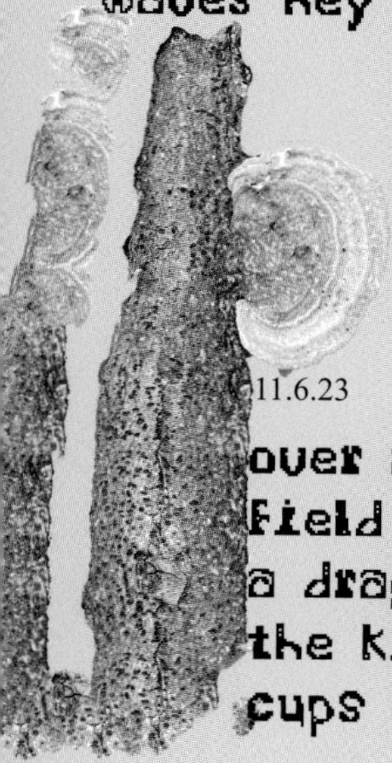

11.6.23

over a perfectly square
field of grass
a dragonfly circles
the kids bring us up
cups of coffee

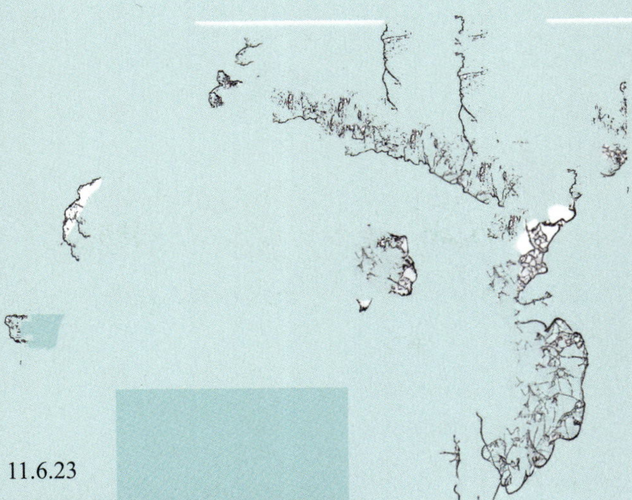

11.6.23

heldere zomerdag
onder het dak van een boom
priemende bladeren
wie voorbij komt
zwaait hey hey!

11.6.23

boven een perfect vierkant
grasveld
cirkelt een libelle
de kinderen brengen ons
kopjes koffie

11.6.23

diagonal trees
resting on each other
fingers rubbing bark
the sound of a grass blade
blown between two thumbs

11.6.23

dry leaves
under my shoes
a crisp sandwich
she makes pancakes
for her grumpy son

11.6.23

bark graffiti
lost in translation
hunebed 21
I go to Japan
to find my stretch marks

11.6.23

diagonale bomen
rusten op elkaar
vingers wrijven over schors
het geluid van een grasspriet
geblazen tussen twee duimen

11.6.23

droge bladeren
onder mijn schoenen
een knapperige sandwich
ze maakt pannenkoeken
voor haar chagrijnige zoon

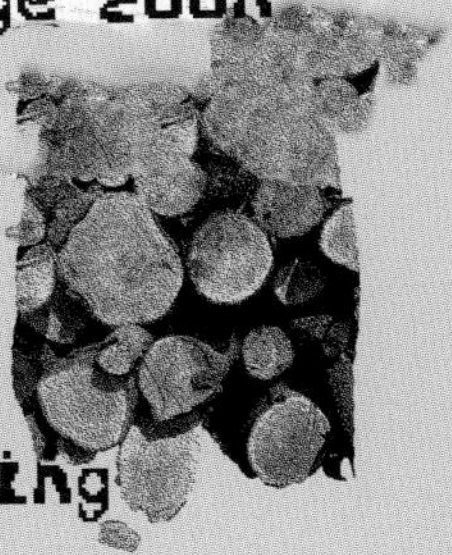

11.6.23

schorsgraffiti
verloren in vertaling
hunebed 21
ik ga naar Japan
om mijn striae te vinden

11.6.23

sunburn
small quick grey spiders
shelter in the cracks
there's always
another boat

11.6.23

old corpses rot
no wonder Bashō
has the stench of zen
wild grasses
on the burial mound

11.6.23

larch tree
what does it look like
from your top?
Noor's kettingzaag
runs out of diesel

11.6.23

zonnebrand
snelle kleine grijze spinnen
schuilen in de kieren
er gaat altijd
een andere boot

11.6.23

oude lijken rotten
geen wonder dat Bashō
de stank van zen heeft
wilde grassen
op de grafheuvel

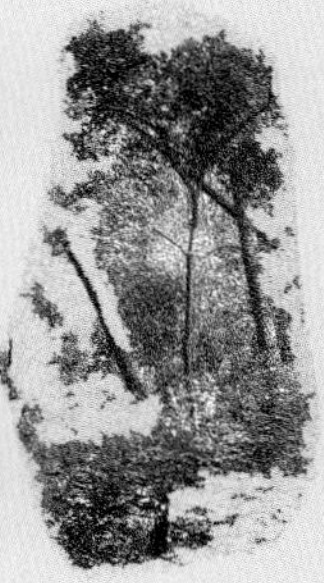

11.6.23

lariksboom
hoe ziet het eruit
vanaf jouw top?
Noors kettingzaag
heeft geen diesel meer

11.6.23

picking off old bark
the remains of pine
just words on paper
familiar bodies
of all shapes

11.6.23

counting birds
water is moving
underground
a stream of leaves
carried by the wind

11.6.23

eat when hungry
and clean your bowl
waiting for interruption
blue skies
will pass too

11.6.23

afplukken van oude schors
de resten van dennen
enkel woorden op papier
vertrouwde lichamen
in alle vormen

11.6.23

vogels tellen
water beweegt
onder de grond
een stroom van bladeren
gedragen door de wind

11.6.23

eet als je honger hebt
en maak je kom schoon
wachten op onderbreking
blauwe luchten
gaan ook voorbij

11.6.23

bramble flowers
a man on a bicycle
spits out a fly
in the mountains
Icarus waters his fig tree

11.6.23

seeking shade
we don't want to mess about
with pregnant women
the butcher sells
bouquets today

11.6.23

small white flowers
stretching over
dead leaves
her mother tells her where
to find her funeral plan

11.6.23

braamstruiken
een man op een fiets
spuugt een vlieg uit
in de bergen
bewatert Icarus zijn vijgenboom

11.6.23

schaduw zoeken
met zwangere vrouwen
we willen niet klooien
de slager verkoopt
boeketten vandaag

11.6.23

kleine witte bloemen
strekken over
dode bladeren
haar moeder vertelt haar waar
haar begrafenisplan ligt

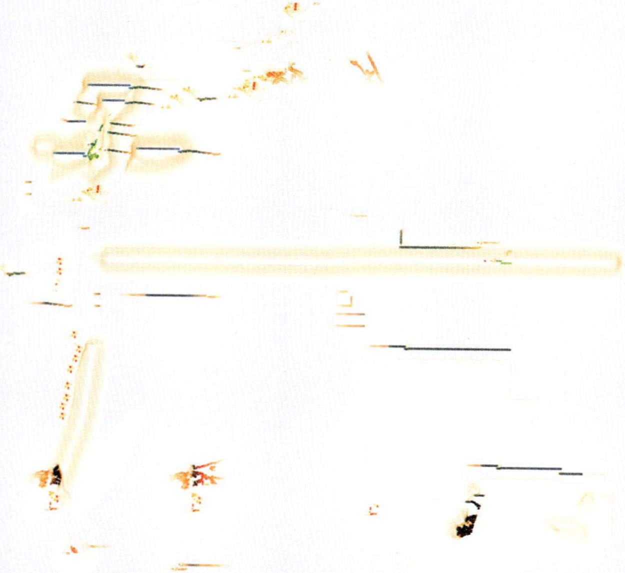

11.6.23

melting ice forms
on the face of the earth
two men love seven
bright open spots
in the arid wood

11.6.23

smeltende ijsvormen
op het aardoppervlak
twee mannen houden van zeven
heldere open plekken
in het dorre bos

11.6.23

the land the time
two points expanding
within parallel lines
I always wanted
two horizons

11.6.23

the earth here
has a strange smell
honouring what came before
middle day sunshine
grounds the leaves

11.6.23

polychronic trees
living and dying
in the summer heat
a beetle without a book
eating the pattern of time

11.6.23

het land de tijd
twee punten breiden zich uit
binnen parallelle lijnen
ik wilde altijd al
twee horizons

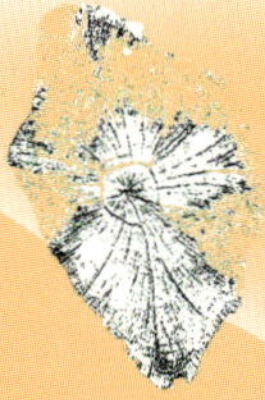

11.6.23

de aarde hier
heeft een vreemde geur
eren wat hiervoor kwam
middagzon
grondt de bladeren

11.6.23

polychrone bomen
leven en sterven
in de zomerhitte
een kever zonder boek
eet het patroon van de tijd

11.6.23

such a relief
not to be guilty
of metaphors
please let me hide
under your dress

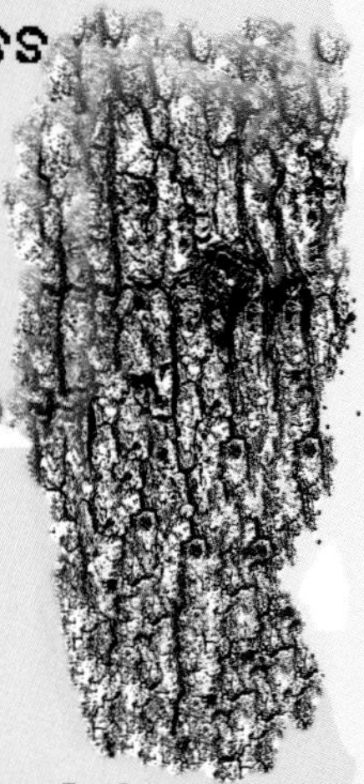

11.6.23

hairy leaves
rustling in the cool breeze
beech and stone joined
on their first flight abroad
all the men wear ties

11.6.23

wat een opluchting
om niet schuldig te zijn
aan metaforen
laat me me verstoppen
onder je jurk

11.6.23

harige bladeren
ritselend in de koele bries
beuk en steen verenigd
op hun eerste vliegreis
dragen alle mannen een stropdas

11.6.23

the story of the earth
shadows of men in the woods
explaining with their hands
procreation
and having sex

11.6.23

the sound of a bird
black lines in the sky
white curtains
the pig farmer erects
a fat dirty fence

11.6.23

shadows play
across grave stones
a crow caws twice
one long log
one short

11.6.23

het verhaal van de aarde
schaduwen van mannen in het bos
die met hun handen uitleggen
voortplanting
en seks hebben

11.6.23

het geluid van een vogel
zwarte lijnen in de lucht
witte gordijnen
de varkensboer trekt
een vet vies hek op

11.6.23

schaduwen spelen
over grafstenen
een kraai kraait twee keer
één lange boomstam
één korte

11.6.23

told not to stray
from the woodland path
we become squirrels
my mother tries
to feed me candy

11.6.23

hunebed 21
the ancient beech speaks
of love that grows
together the sparrows
make one hell of a noise

11.6.23

warm smell of wood
a soft summer breeze
surrounding home
this land dishonoured
again and again

11.6.23

gezegd niet af te dwalen
van het bospad
we worden eekhoorns
mijn moeder probeert
me snoep te voeren

11.6.23

hunebed 21
de oude beuk spreekt
van liefde die groeit
samen maken de mussen
een hels kabaal

11.6.23

de warme geur van hout
een zacht zomerbriesje
omringt thuis
dit land onteerd
opnieuw en opnieuw

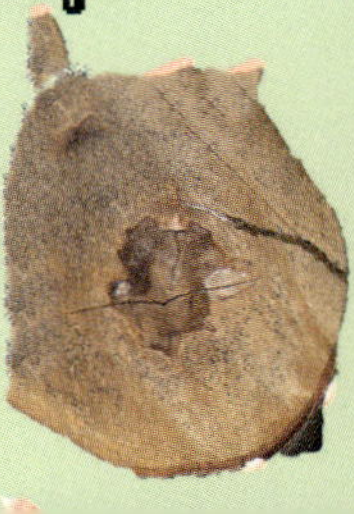

11.6.23

little mountain peaks
where the saw
doesn't reach
an open door says
let's go to the beach

11.6.23

back and forth
seven evocations
like swirling stories
I translate a fugue
and stumble

11.6.23

kleine bergtoppen
waar de zaag
niet reikt
een open deur zegt
laten we naar het strand gaan

11.6.23

heen en weer
zeven evocaties
als wervelende verhalen
ik vertaal een fuga
en struikel

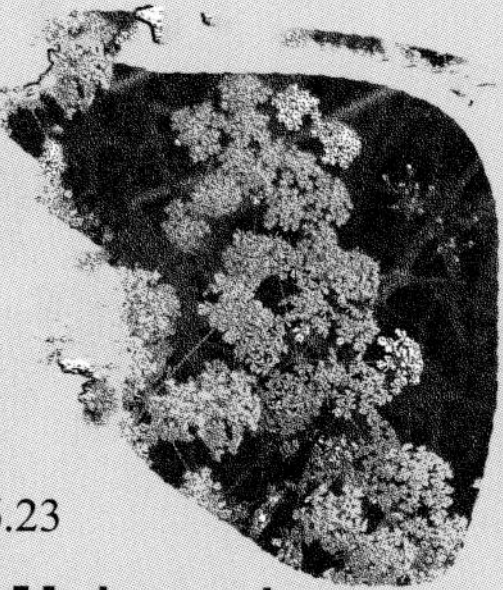

11.6.23

walking into
the sound of birds
a fallen pine
hearing you cry
for the first time

11.6.23

rustling leaves
between standing statues
countless figures
paying for the excess
on my new windscreen

11.6.23

wandelen in
het geluid van vogels
een omgevallen den
je horen huilen
voor het eerst

11.6.23

ritselende bladeren
tussen staande beelden
ontelbare figuren
betalen voor het teveel
op mijn nieuwe voorruit

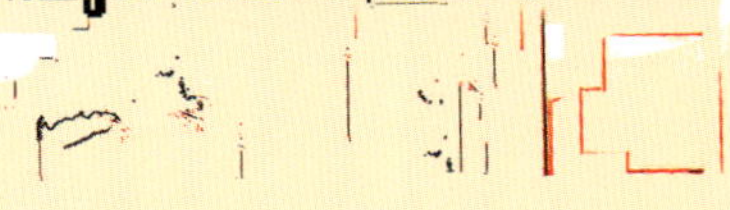

11.6.23

the sun moves
in all of us
bodies in the outer land
there are never too many
reruns of Logan's Run

11.6.23

the restlessness
of burning flowers
summer evil
anti aircraft guns
in a field of barley

11.6.23

capture a moment
a half hearted man in
automatic portrait mode
if I must write
let it be in silence

11.6.23

de zon beweegt
in ons allemaal
lichamen in het land hier buiten
er zijn nooit te veel
herhalingen van Logan's Run

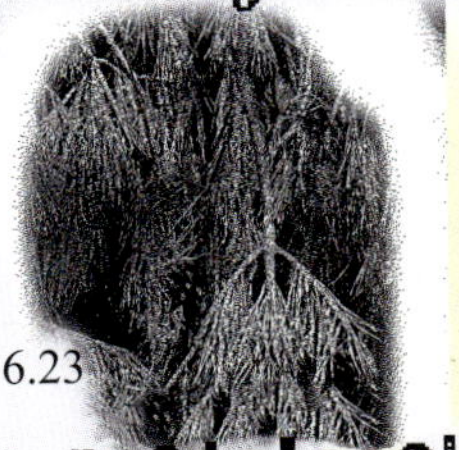

11.6.23

de rusteloosheid
van brandende bloemen
's zomers kwaad
luchtafweergeschut
in een veld met gerst

11.6.23

leg een moment vast
een halfhartige man in
automatische portretmodus
als ik moet schrijven
laat het in stilte zijn

11.6.23

100 birds
the shaded seat
half way down the path
the sound of your hair
being brushed

11.6.23

a green curtain
sprouting on dry soil
gushes of wind
kids running back and forth
under the garden sprinkler

11.6.23

a young woman falls
between the pine trees
her bottom becomes one
two boys race
on the count of three

11.6.23

100 vogels
de schaduwrijke zitplaats
halverwege het pad
het geluid van je haar
dat geborsteld wordt

11.6.23

een groen gordijn
ontspruit op droge grond
windvlagen
kinderen rennen heen en weer
onder de tuinsproeier

11.6.23

een jonge vrouw zit
tussen de naaldbomen
haar billen en hout worden één
twee jongens racen
op de tel van drie

11.6.23

gushes of wind
a loud chitter chatter
passes time
Mr Bang Bang
goes to meet the giants

11.6.23

trying out
some hazelnut spread
on my knäckebröd
reaching my lips
and then crack!

11.6.23

bramble bush blossoms
my shoes
patterned with scratches
Rose dances the Robot
on the church floor

11.6.23

windvlagen
een luid gebabbel
doet tijd verstrijken
Mr Bang Bang
gaat de reuzen ontmoeten

11.6.23

probeer
wat hazelnootpasta
op mijn knäckebröd
bereik mijn lippen
en dan krak!

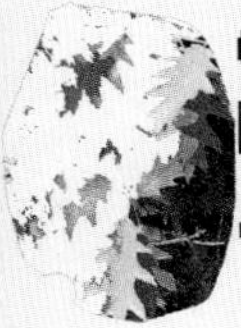

11.6.23

braamstruik bloesem
mijn schoenen
met krassen versierd
Roos danst de Robot
op de kerkvloer

11.6.23

a path is left
your hear it
by its open shape
mowing out
May's wild meadow

11.6.23

whistling flower
a large wooden wall
in a dip
the school sets a limit
on red and brown sauce

11.6.23

een pad is verlaten
je hoort het
door zijn open vorm
het wegmaaien van
mei's wilde weide

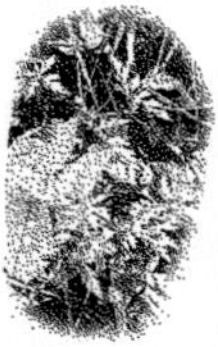

11.6.23

fluitende bloem
een grote houten wand
in een kuil
de school stelt een limiet
aan rode en bruine saus

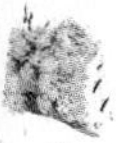

11.6.23

one word
changing stuff
to honour it
I keep
a multiverse

10.6.23

log after log
resisting the urge
to turn one over
on the other hand
more words

10.6.23

taking up speed
under the moon
busy tourist tractor
a painted stag
escapes the wolf pack

11.6.23

één woord
verandert vanalles
om het te eren
bewaar ik
een multiversum

10.6.23

blok na blok
weerstand bieden aan de drang
om er een om te draaien
aan de andere kant
meer woorden

10.6.23

snelheid maken
onder de maan
drukke toeristische trekker
een geverfd hert
ontvlucht de wolvenroedel

10.6.23

the submission
when did we stop
being part of nature?
in the hanging gardens
I find time to take a selfie

10.6.23

a conversation
with a wanderer
isn't it artistic?
I try to remember
my father's voice

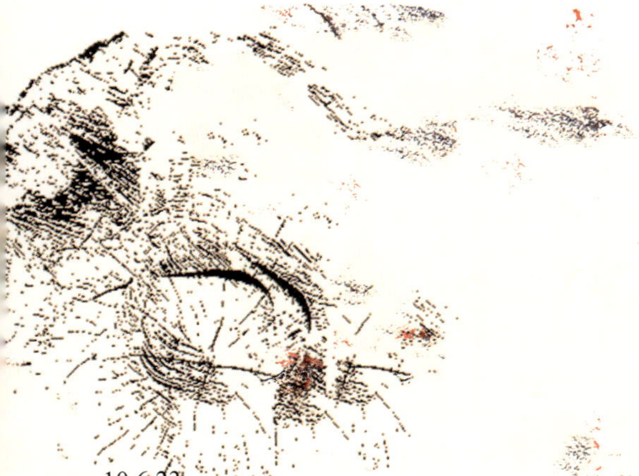

10.6.23

de onderwerping
wanneer zijn we gestopt
deel te zijn van de natuur?
in de hangende tuinen
vind ik tijd voor een selfie

10.6.23

een gesprek
met een dwaler
is het niet artistiek?
mijn vaders stem
poog ik te herinneren

10.6.23

the exploitation
of endless walking
chopped trees
Hilde finds
a comfy seat

10.6.23

shadows of leaves
on paper
poems in the constant sun
a morning spent
walking the forest

10.6.23

bark graffiti
turns beech into oak
the sun burns
all the little grains
sticking to her skin

10.6.23

de uitbuiting
van eindeloos lopen
gekapte bomen
Hilde vindt
een comfortabel zitje

10.6.23

schaduwen van bladeren
op papier
verzen in de constante zon
een ochtend doorgebracht
wandelend door het bos

10.6.23

schorsgraffiti
verandert beuk in eik
de zon verbrandt
alle kleine korrels
die aan haar huid kleven

8.6.23

four times a year
help me to express
this feeling of change
taking a shower to clean
not to just warm up

7.6.23

just before dinner
I water the allotment
green beans and leeks
an environmental bomb
of mass destruction

7.6.23

Hollander beaters
coniferous pulp
rolled dried and heated
the ink pen's nib
against fine paper

8.6.23

viermaal per jaar
help me uiting te geven
aan het gevoel van verandering
een douche nemen
niet alleen om op te warmen

7.6.23

vlak voor het avondeten
geef ik de volkstuin water
sperziebonen en prei
een milieubom
van massavernietiging

7.6.23

Hollander beaters
naaldhoutpulp
gerold gedroogd en verwarmd
de punt van de inktpen
tegen fijn papier

7.6.23

the copper angels
whistling
up the copper tree
she thinks to herself there are
too many pipes in this house

6.6.23

not able
to hide her tears
a veil of daisies
inside his walking cane
the polished blade

5.6.23

planting seeds
under a strawberry moon
dirt under my nails
fumbling in the dark
binoculars and iPhone

7.6.23

de koperen engelen
fluitend
in de koperen boom
ze denkt bij zichzelf er zijn
te veel leidingen in dit huis

6.6.23

niet in staat
haar tranen te verbergen
een sluier van madeliefjes
in zijn wandelstok
het gepolijste lemmet

5.6.23

zaden planten
onder een aardbeienmaan
vuil onder mijn nagels
rommelen in het donker
verrekijker en iPhone

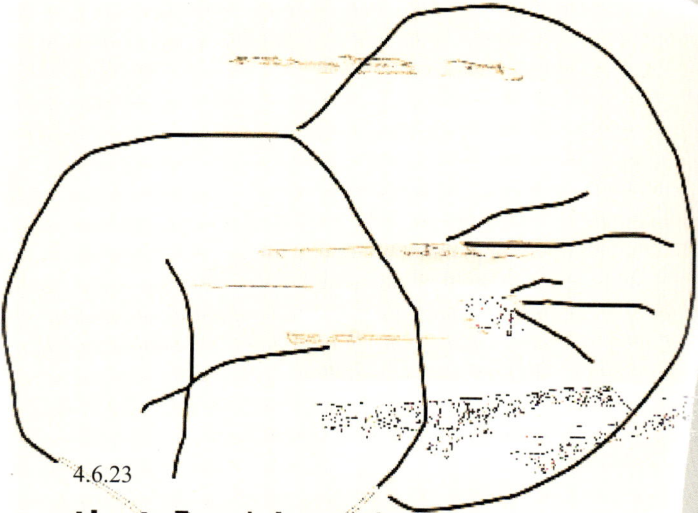

4.6.23

that Druids stick
leaning against the wall
it's mine now
finders keepers
losers weepers

31.5.23

imaginary texts
Bashō asks us both
a difficult question
huge red poppies
in a field of wheat

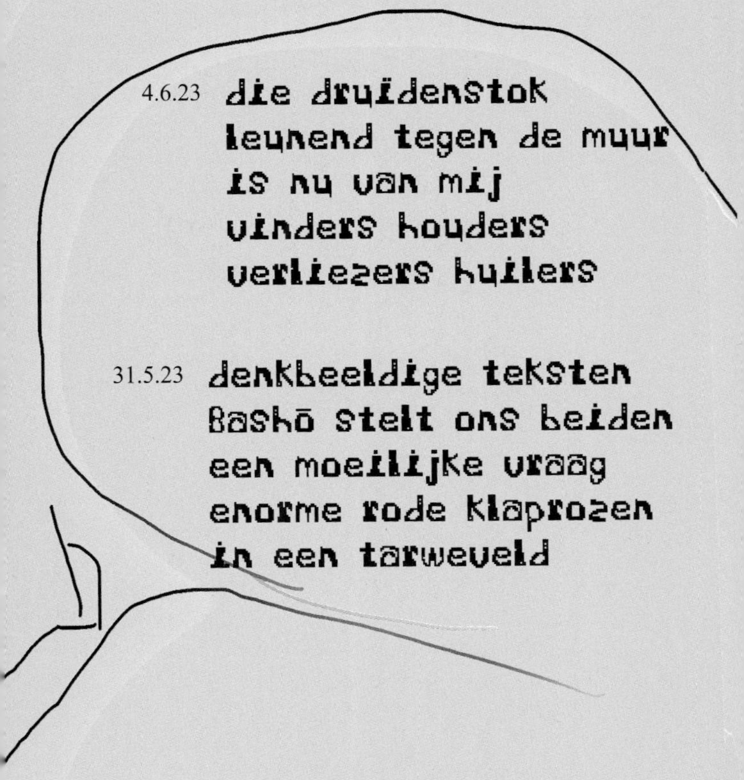

4.6.23 die druidenstok
leunend tegen de muur
is nu van mij
vinders houders
verliezers huilers

31.5.23 denkbeeldige teksten
Bashō stelt ons beiden
een moeilijke vraag
enorme rode klaprozen
in een tarweveld

30.5.23

sixty thousand tons
of unsold clothes dumped
in the Atacama Desert
dad wonders who taught mum
to tango like that?

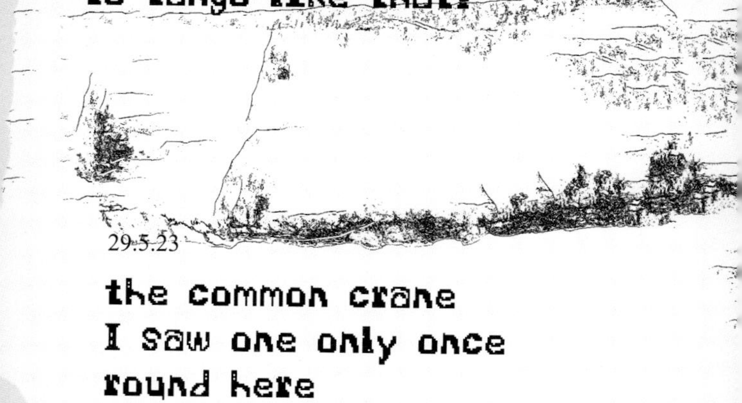

29.5.23

the common crane
I saw one only once
round here
even as a baby
he had long legs

30.5.23

zestigduizend ton
onverkochte kleding gedumpt
in de Atacama woestijn
vader vraagt wie moeder
leerde om zo te tangoën

29.5.23

de kraanvogel
ik zag er ooit eens één
in deze buurt
zelfs als baby
had hij lange poten

29.5.23

Fireworks over Kiev
insecure Russians
and Iranian drones
a stairwell piled high
with blood and rubble

27.5.23 our Celestial Empire
possesses all things
in prolific abundance
the woman at check in
tells me I'm overweight

29.5.23

vuurwerk boven Kiev
onzekere Russen
en Iraanse drones
een trappenhuis volgestapeld
met bloed en puin

27.5.23

ons Hemelse Rijk
bezit alle dingen
in vruchtbare overvloed
de vrouw bij het inchecken
zegt dat ik overgewicht heb

27.5.23

silver lady
a lungful of David Soul
and micro plastics
as night falls the saguaro
opens its stomata

27.5.23

that smell
that flavour
blowing up a lilo
ground breathing above
and below sea level

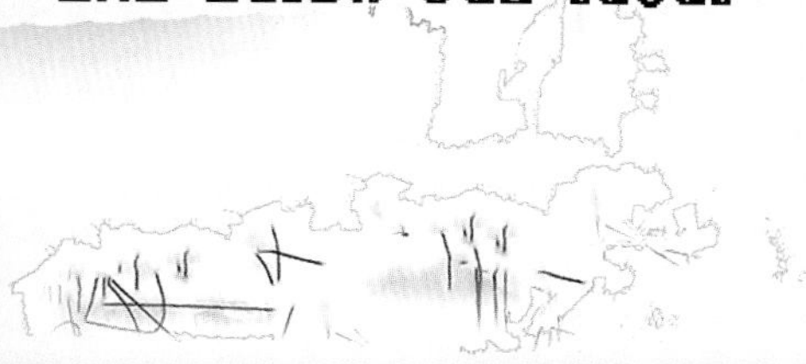

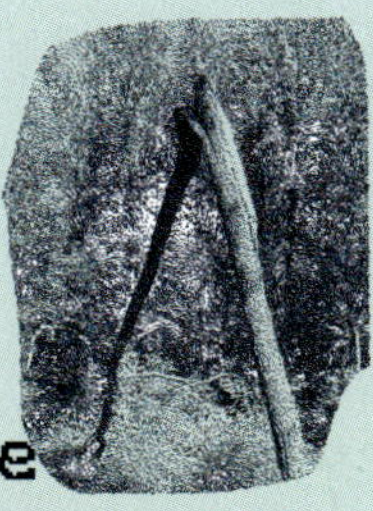

27.5.23

zilveren dame
een long vol David Soul
en microplastic
als de avond valt opent
de saguaro zijn poriën

27.5.23

die geur
die smaak
een luchtbed opblazen
grond ademt boven
en onder zeeniveau

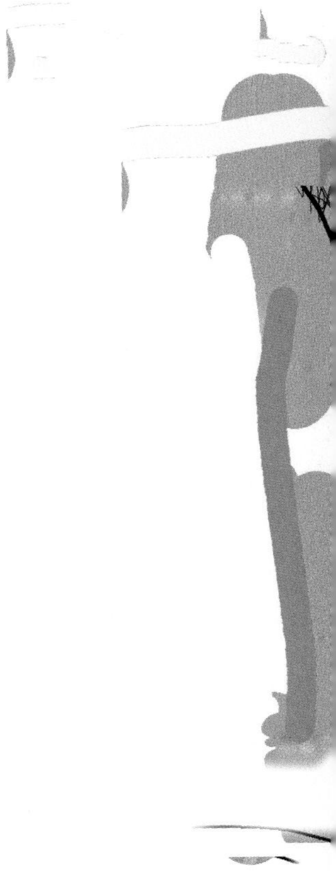

Published by Set Margins'
www.setmargins.press
ISBN: 978-90-833188-8-2
first edition, 2023

Made possible thanks to the generous support of
Into Nature, The Culture & Nature Network,
We the North, De Versterking,
and Birmingham City University.

Special thanks to Hilde de Bruijn, Freek Lomme,
Sian Vaughan, Etel Adnan, and Adrienne Wade, Red Wade
and Orlando Wade.

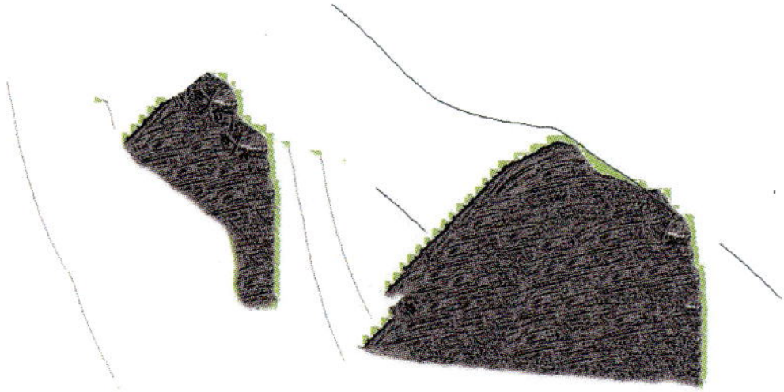

Set Margins' #12

Is this the way the universe works? (77 Verses / 555 Verses)

Gavin Wade and Paul Conneally

Graphic design by James Langdon
Verse typeface by Mohammad Al Hayo
Type-size-by-surface-area processing by Simon Knebl

Print production coordinated by Trudy Dorrepaal

Photography by Gavin Wade
Image processing by James Langdon

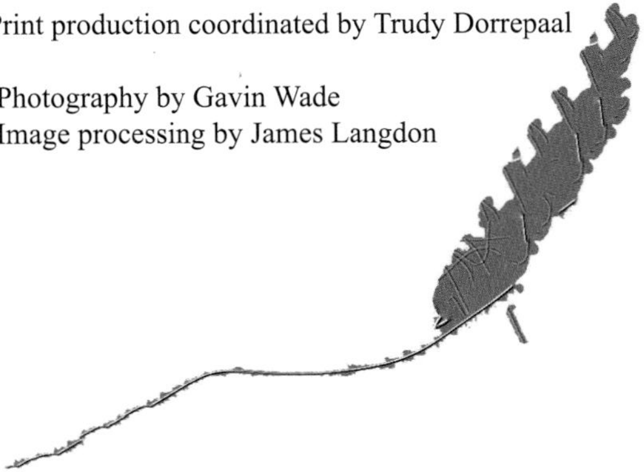

Gavin Wade (he/him)
Lives and works in Birmingham, UK.

Gavin Wade is an artist-curator, pragmatic utopian and serial collaborator. His practice combines upcycling, re-enactment and developing exhibiting structures for supporting the work of others. Gavin is a founder of, and co-runs, artist-run-multiverse Eastside Projects since 2008; is Senior Research Fellow at Birmingham City University; maker and curator of world-class public art, exhibition making, writing, music and publishing over the last two decades; and collaborates with his horticulturist wife Adrienne Wade on Triangle Garden, an exotic garden at their home in Birmingham.

Gavin learned the renga form from artists Alec Finlay and Paul Conneally while making *100 Verses for 3 Estates* (Strategic Questions, 2007) as part of a year-long public art commission. Since then he has developed a deep collaboration with Conneally, creating #tantwenga and eleven 100 verse #twenga poems (with up to 18 writers) as a shared open workshop published using @eprjcts Twitter platform as well as making music together.

His song *66 Verses (Once I moved about like the wind)* and albums *Songs of the Modern World,* volumes 1 and 2 (and 3 forthcoming) on New Reality Records are available on most music platforms, and his many books include *Upcycle This Book* (2017) and *Has Man A Function In Universe?* (2008), both designed by collaborator James Langdon and published by Book Works.

Paul Conneally (he/him)

Lives and works in Loughbohemia
(some call it Loughborough), UK.

Paul Conneally is a cultural forager, poet, artist and musician. He founded New Reality Records in 2020.

Conneally's work has the haikai process of link and shift running through it, a constant thread being the art of surprising comparison and an endeavour to wherever possible show-not-tell. He has been a leading haikai poet over the last three decades, and has been described by the Embassy of Japan in the UK as an "experienced expert" in the field of haiku and led many haiku workshops for teachers on behalf of the embassy and Japan 21.

Conneally is also known variously as Little Onion and papà caos amongst other names.

Matsuo Bashō is the most famous Japanese writer of all time. Living between 1644 and 1694 he attracted many disciples and associates with his mastering of linked verse renga poetry, the poetic diary form Haibun, and his development of the single form poetry hokku which we now call haiku. He was honoured and canonised as a deity on the hundredth anniversary of his death. He alone is known as a haisei, the saint of haiku. He is known to have lived a simple life, walking and writing, resting in huts his students built for him, being invited by people to perform and write renga with them. His work Narrow Road to the Interior recounts his last long walk, from May to September 1689, of 1,200 miles.

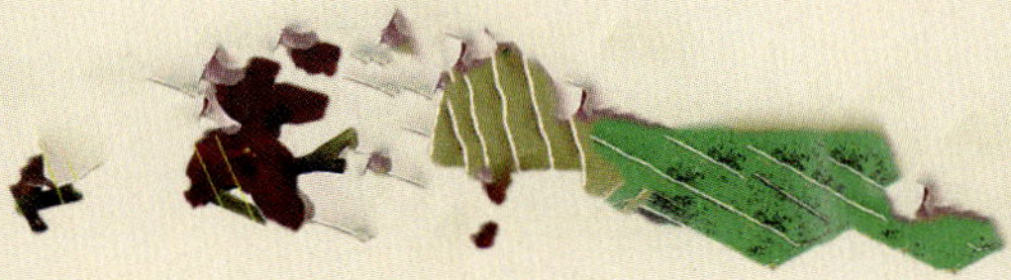

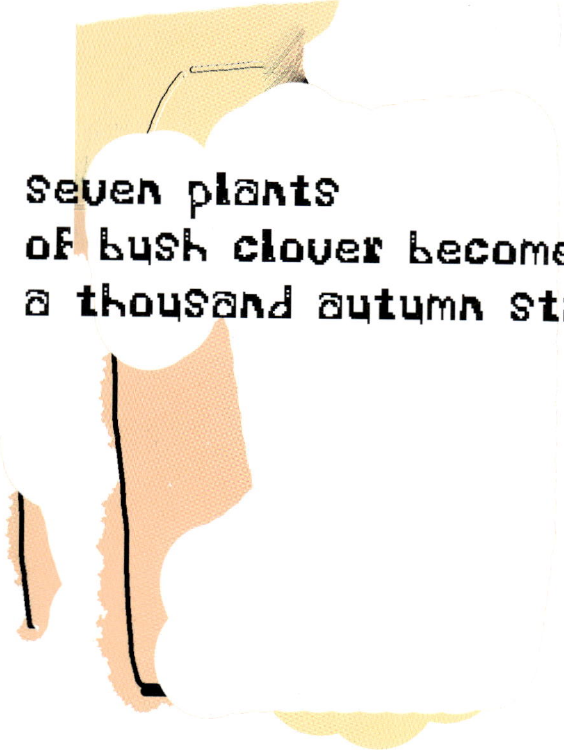

seven plants
of bush clover become
a thousand autumn stars

Bashō: To celebrate Tanabata and the seventy seven years of Sodo's mother, I was one of seven poets who chose each of the seven autumn plants as a theme for single verses, wishing ourselves also to live as old as the seven old Chinese poets:

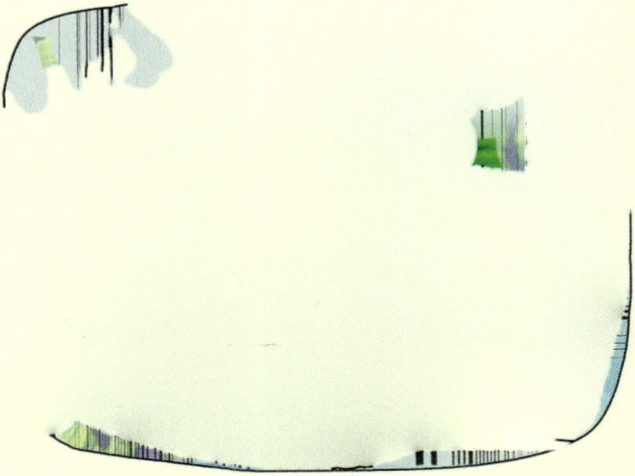

Paul: Maybe it's best to leave our thoughts out of it. Let the trees talk.

Bashō: The vicissitudes of life are swift, and life is ephemeral.

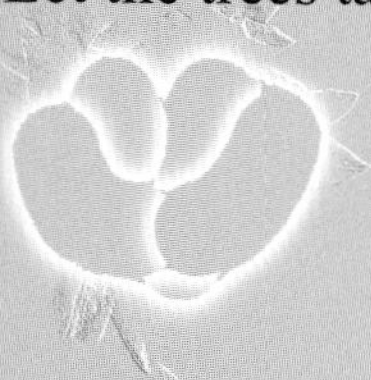

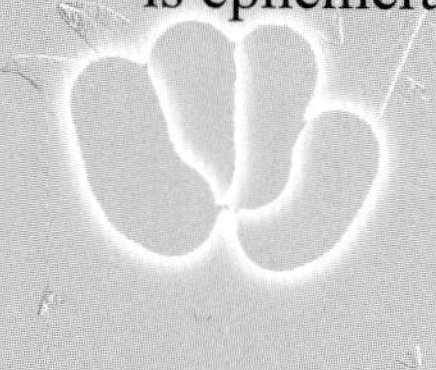

Gavin: Yes, OK. We will get on with it. No time to waste. Us two mortals have got plenty to do but I suppose this is a moment also to celebrate, a moment where our verses land and connect with the ground, the trees, the grass and the insects and hopefully people who pass through these woods, and perhaps even wolves, this quite wonderful place.

Paul: Hera spraying milk across the sky.

Bashō: Matsushima is known as the most beautiful place in Japan. Since olden times, it has been depicted in poetry and pictures by many poets and artists. It has an expanse of about seven miles of sea coast, where there are many offshore islands carved into various shapes by the wind and waves. Many of the islands, or sea stacks, have enough soil to support a few wind bent pines, making them seem to be stages for a play about the gods.

many islands
broken into pieces
summer's sea

Gavin: A play about the gods? OK. So much to think about.

Bashō:

logged tree
the larger cut end
a harvest moon

Gavin: You see the moon in everything?

Bashō: I see everything in the moon.

Paul: And what do you see in the pines?

Bashō: Glimmers.

Gavin: These 77 logs will be moved again when 77 new trees are planted around the wood in November. I imagine the logs to be companions, accents, little links and shifts to and from the newly planted trees. Perhaps it is 77 of our verses that are the companions for the trees? 555 companions for the visitors, the readers, the carriers of these verses.

even woodpeckers
do not damage this hut
a summer grove

Paul: I can't stop thinking about bananas – Mona Lisa, Ice Cream and Goldfinger.

Gavin: Bananas and your huts Bashō. Real and unreal. What a way to live. Moving from hut to hut. No belongings.

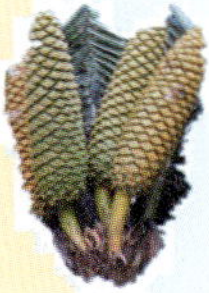

A true lightness. Hard to achieve. We will make piles of cut and carved logs. Carved with verses in them. Seven verses in seven types of tree cut down, into logs – ash, lime, elder, maple, silver birch, oak and of course pine.

Gavin: A difficult ask. For me. Here in Drenthe we are making some places to sit and read verses, of this place, and connections to other places and people around the world. Verses Paul and I have formed over the last six years. We can sit together on these logs. Imagine if in each log there was a book of verses to pull out and read outloud.

Bashō:

less than five foot square
grass shelter not needed
unless there is rain

I understand that the Priest Butcho composed this poem about his home here. Seeing this place is so much more impressive than hearing about it, and I feel my heart is purified.

earliest spring
selling plum flower wine
the fragrance

Gavin: This is the way the universe works.

Bashō: Eating what was given, and what I begged for, surviving without starving, till the end of the year:

perhaps I'll be one
of those happy people
old at the years end

Gavin: I think I am beginning to appreciate this verse more now Bashō.

Bashō: A motto: Do not mention the faults of others. Do not mention one's own merits.

a dragonfly
unable to settle
on the grass

in our #tantwenga, words composed just five years ago, also in Autumn:

a moth egg laid
in the influorescence
of an aged yucca
if you find the Buddha
kill the Buddha

Bashō: There lived a man at Take no Uchi in Kazuraki County. He took good care of his family, employing many workers who plowed the paddy fields in spring and harvested rice in autumn. His house was filled with the scent of plum blossoms, which encouraged and consoled sorrowful poets.

Paul: It's a herb. The banana plant. That always surprises people. Surprised me anyway.

Bashō: Aha. Tell me how you are adding to the evolution of haikai, of poetry, of art, of everything?

Gavin:
By clinging on
for dear life!

Paul: By looking backwards to move forwards. Sideways too. Embracing the new and returning to the old. Oscillating. Walking the borders.

Gavin: Great words Paul. Okay, how else to see-through-words in this digital world? In your own words Bashō, written 333 years ago this Autumn:

Paul:

three names
in a wine glass
one tree

Bashō: The basho's useless nature is itself reason to admire it. The monk Huaisu lovingly followed the bark with his brush to learn its ways. The astronomer, mathematician and poet Zhang Heng watched the leaves unfold to inspire his studies. I am like neither. I rest in the shade of the basho leaves, because they are so easily torn.

Paul: I just planted a small banana plant in my back garden…

Gavin: Our Musa basjoos are shooting up huge new leaves at the moment about twelve feet tall and one usually flowers each year which is always an event for humans and insects alike.

Bashō: To know of the pine, go to the pine. Of the bamboo, go to the bamboo.

Paul: Is this the way the universe works?

Bashō: Three people living in Reiganjima came to my place late last night. Their names happened to be all the same. This reminded me of Li Po's poem of 'Drinking Alone under the Moon,' and so I playfully composed this verse:

the wine bowl moon
filled full with three names
to drink this evening

Gavin: Well, we don't have the same names but we do all have perfectly bald heads! I hope we have strong links beyond that though and can share this space together, to be with these trees, this land, drink together, breathe the same air.

and You, Me Bashō

Paul: Where are you going?

Bashō: To the pine.

Gavin: Sadly, the pines here in Drenthe are dying. They are being eaten by letterzetters – the European spruce bark beetle (Ips typographus) not the Six toothed bark beetle, although it has a great name too. This was one of the first things that Hilde told me about this wood here in Drenthe. That the pines were being eaten alive, the letterzetters are drawing doodles under the bark of the trees, eating the wood, creating type of a type, laying their larvae and spreading across the forests. I immediately thought of you Bashō, and your many few words.

Gavin: Why?

Bashō: To know of it.

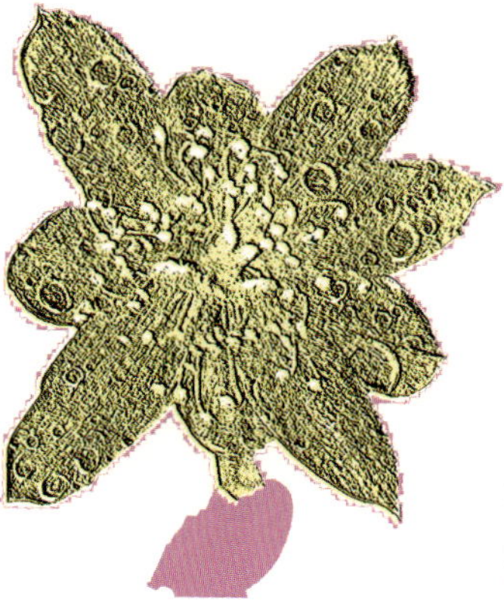

25.2.17

acorns
on the old stone bridge
she fastens his coat
the red squirrel
clings on for dear life

5.3.17

sleeping rough next to
an oligarch's mansion
just for a second
the full moon's
perfect roundness

28.2.17

shameless patch
green spikes tickled
by this tender breeze
the blind man's guide
humping a footstool

6.3.17

gold glitter
all over the stairs
to the designer's studio
a zero hours cleaner
with the face of an angel

5.3.17

getting a feel
for my new impact driver
a day and two nights
wrapped in a hempen quilt
wild asters and nuts

31.3.17

a five minute walk
round and round the house
blackthorn blossom
confusing hand signs
wind up the auctioneer

29.3.17

emergency stents
a big heart is released
from hospital
the white feathered crow
picks through fallen branches

1.4.17

seen from my armchair
so many daytime stars
the greengage in bloom
a smoke trail
over Cadbury World

10.4.17

forget me nots
trying too hard to relax
my angina kicks in
the door opens to
a neighbour carrying gifts

4.4.17

raising beds
with old scaffold planks
daffodil breath
the first ten minute walk
after my heart attack

22.4.17

teenagers share a spliff
in the park bandstand
tulips and pansies
floating down the river
in a bubble

12.4.17

fast flowing water
over a bed of pebbles
air and gas
prefabricated architecture
dropped in by chopper

2.5.17

opening lilac
the feel of the morning sun
on my upturned face
lost in the patterns
of the markings on your skin

23.4.17

I ascend like a dragon
or a brilliant lark
the yew, the oak, the rose
a multitude of cultures
under one flag

4.5.17

Scanning the horizon
for the concave peak
burning calf muscles
a tube of deep heat
and the lark ascending

4.5.17

First election speech
falling like a goat carcass
smacking off concrete
glottal stops and spittle
wrapped in a tissue

13.5.17

pavement blossom
a street sleeper whistles
tulips from Amsterdam
Russian icons above
a De Stijl desk

6.5.17

the stranger leads Vito
down a grimy alley
night time fishing
we follow the reflection
of the moon home

6.5.17

mid morning break
a squirrel with a mouthful
of tulip petals
her first attempt to walk
results in a scream

21.5.17

a pile of red bricks
under a horse chestnut tree
memorial stones
Dad's t-shirt says
the world isn't working

15.5.17

spring lamb
the butcher wipes his hands
down his apron
five a side called off
due to lack of heart

29.5.17

creaking joints
the sound of a long tailed tit
in an old ash tree
burning with ecstasy
on the hot dance floor

28.5.17

the young pharmacist
tells me to 'take care now'
wilting strawberries
blistering feet
shuffling home after dark

14.6.17

in the shower
something brushes my shoulder
playground death
the old man of spring
loosens his beard

5.7.17

cornered eye
the moon outshines
the sons of anarchy
my mother calls me
by my father's name

26.6.17

class war
an unstoppable heron
swallows a duckling live
the rolling news team
hands back to the studio

22.6.17

Burt's bees
the lingering sting
of my wife's kiss
our patch of nettles
crawling with caterpillars

10.7.17

lightning conductors
their deep quiet
restores our hearts
new pumps shoot rainbows
over the pond

8.7.17

just a few beers
on the charabanc home
we follow the moon
ping goes the sat nav
whump goes the clutch

26.7.17

stifling heat
the car park attendant's
rolled up sleeves
skyscrapers sink
into the ground

26.7.17

hearts murmur
a thousand bees
in dad's lavender
the captain switches
to autopilot

26.7.17

skyscrapers sink
into the ground
hearts murmur
a thousand bees
in dad's lavender

9.8.17

inking the plate
a vase full of summer
and paper cut scars
debt rises
and taxes stay low

7.8.17

we meet people
brand new people
like a nuclear bomb
shadows twisting around
undulating forms

31.8.17

feeling the heat
just one cloud
over the courthouse
a hidden message
in the geometric faade

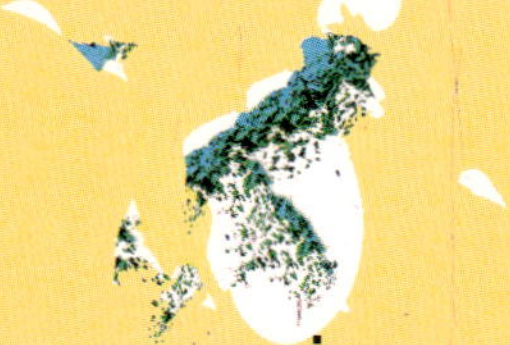

27.8.17

summer pruning
a perfect bird's nest
in the old ivy
cloud formations
define shadow gaps

4.9.17

flickering lights
the sound of someone
gently weeping
the COSHH assessor
recommends a new plan

8.9.17

a portion of sky
caught in a soldier's buckle
his last letter home
a plea from Desmond Tutu
to Aung San Suu Kyi

6.9.17

sucked and popped
dropping cherry stones
on Digbeth's cobbles
the streetworker buys
the street sleeper a coffee

25.9.18

a snow goose
in a field of wheat
passing cars
tearing down
posters spreading hate

17.9.18

stuck in the gap
between my front teeth
summer's end
her whistleblowing
starts a riot

14.9.17

the well fed pigeon
flies through the apple tree
on a day for gloves
the gap between things
becomes nothing

29.9.17

after the school dance
a quick kiss and a fumble
the shape of gravestones
a green void awaiting
a mega station

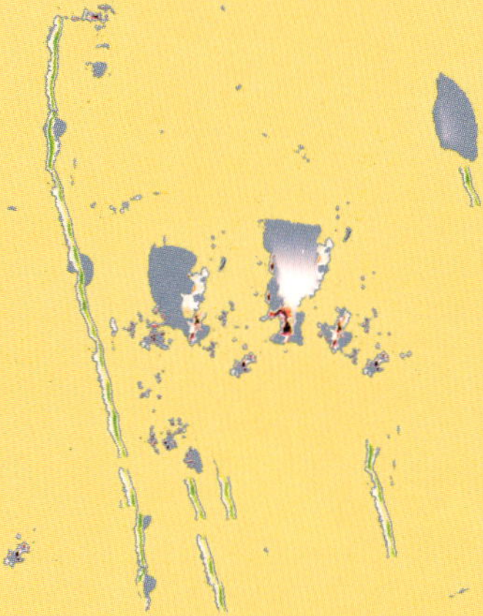

6.10.17

the traffic warden
takes out his notebook
pied wagtails
fingers stretched and ready
awaiting pain

5.10.17

his cremation
a plume of hot air
and handshakes
beans on toast
with a cold glass of milk

16.10.17

sinusitis
a bag of bruised apples
by the fruit press
the wind drowns out
her inner ear's endless gig

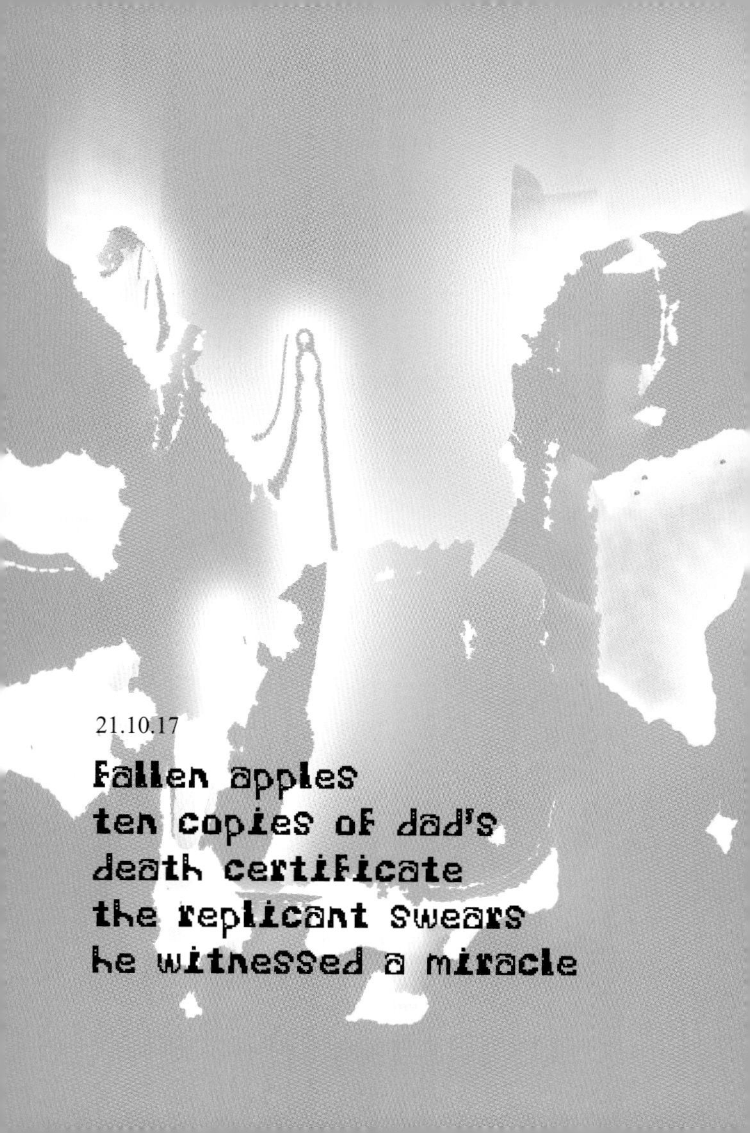

21.10.17

fallen apples
ten copies of dad's
death certificate
the replicant swears
he witnessed a miracle

29.11.17

deepening winter
an intercontinental
ballistic missile
washing out the stains
on his underpants

4.11.17

November wasp
clinging to the glass
watching the humans eat
a bonfire toffee puts paid
to mum's double filling

5.12.17

prizes aren't prizes
when conditions reflect
the bottom of the pile
a sock that was lost
fifteen years ago

5.12.17

a rising tide
lifts all the boats
crab lines
shifting sideways
through the CCTV loop

25.12.17

coming to terms
with the nightclub in my head
sparrows and starlings
swaying eucalyptus limbs
through new binoculars

16.12.17

melting snow
we sit starving
amidst our gold
the jogger's assets
rise and fall

25.3.18

sunrise and sunset
cracking creaking and rumbling
the Moon never rests
stretching weary limbs
the pack prepare to hunt

23.3.18

blowing volcanic sand
out of my snorkel
the whole morning spent
talking with flowers
no more self doubts

14.4.18

after the storm
a child picking spring flowers
from a bomb crater
please make your way
to outpatients

25.3.18

the bowler's secret
hidden in his underpants
a piece of rough tape
marking the boundaries
of the factory floor

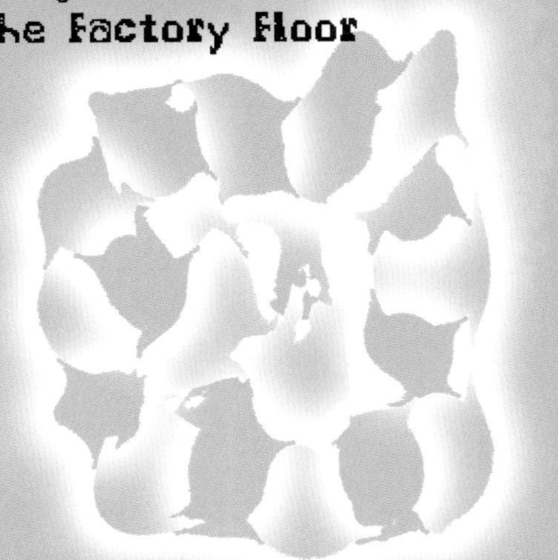

5.5.18

at the art fair
eyes caught by a girl
in red high heels
a virus multiplying
through your bloodstream

21.4.18

distant air strikes
an agave needle
sticking in my knee
acupuncture and codeine
will cure anything

21.4.18

kahu huruhuru
soaring above the world
looking for a nest
a dunnock sitting
on a cuckoo's egg

8.5.18

deep asleep
under a chestnut tree
the butcher's dog
held by the circi
of an irate earwig

5.5.18

stinging nettles
a dock leaf held tight
to my left arm
wax and paper
wrapping the gravestone

12.5.18

clematis
a tingling from left foot
to left ear
she tells an old joke
about a motherfucker

8.5.18

UV approved
quickly reconditioning
too tight head barrels
the band beats out a cycle
of fourths and fifths

25.5.18

protection racket
Russian jobs deemed
too dangerous for women
it's one set all
and everything to play for

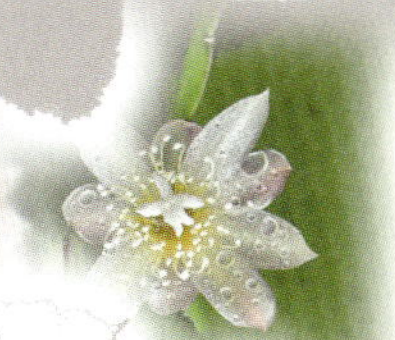

17.5.18

stopping to gaze
at flags in the border
the smell of bacon
washed so softly
by the Cornish surf

27.5.18

beautiful people
sing their own songs
crochets and quavers
not the right to buy
but the right to knit

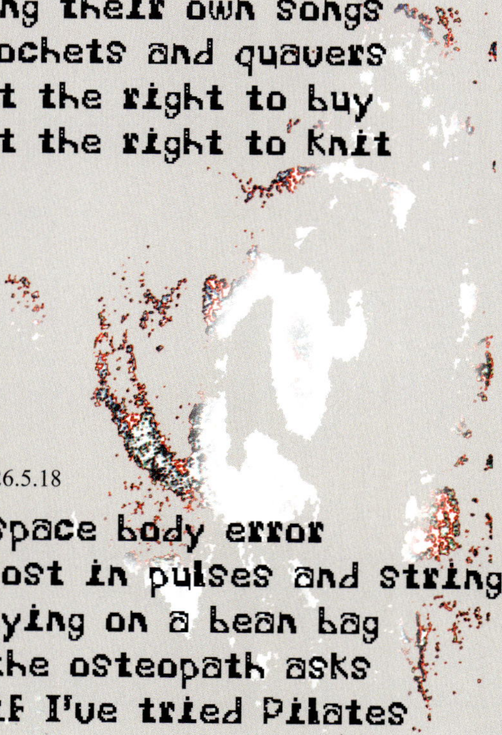

26.5.18

space body error
lost in pulses and strings
lying on a bean bag
the osteopath asks
if I've tried Pilates

29.5.18

from her high rise
she takes in the city
another reality
peoples pay gradually
becomes universal

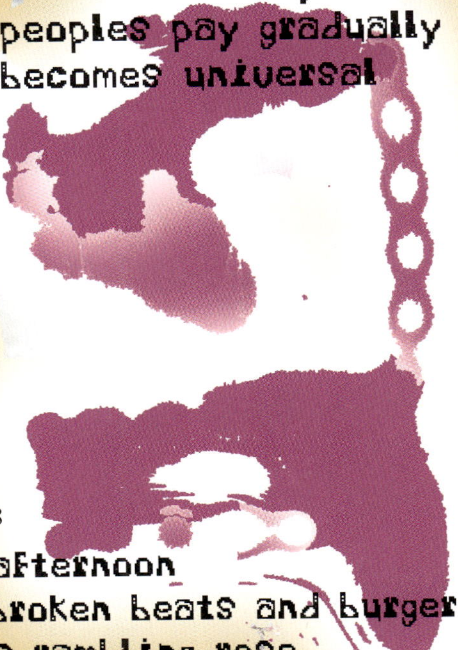

28.5.18

an afternoon
of broken beats and burgers
this rambling rose
washing school uniforms
and providing tampons

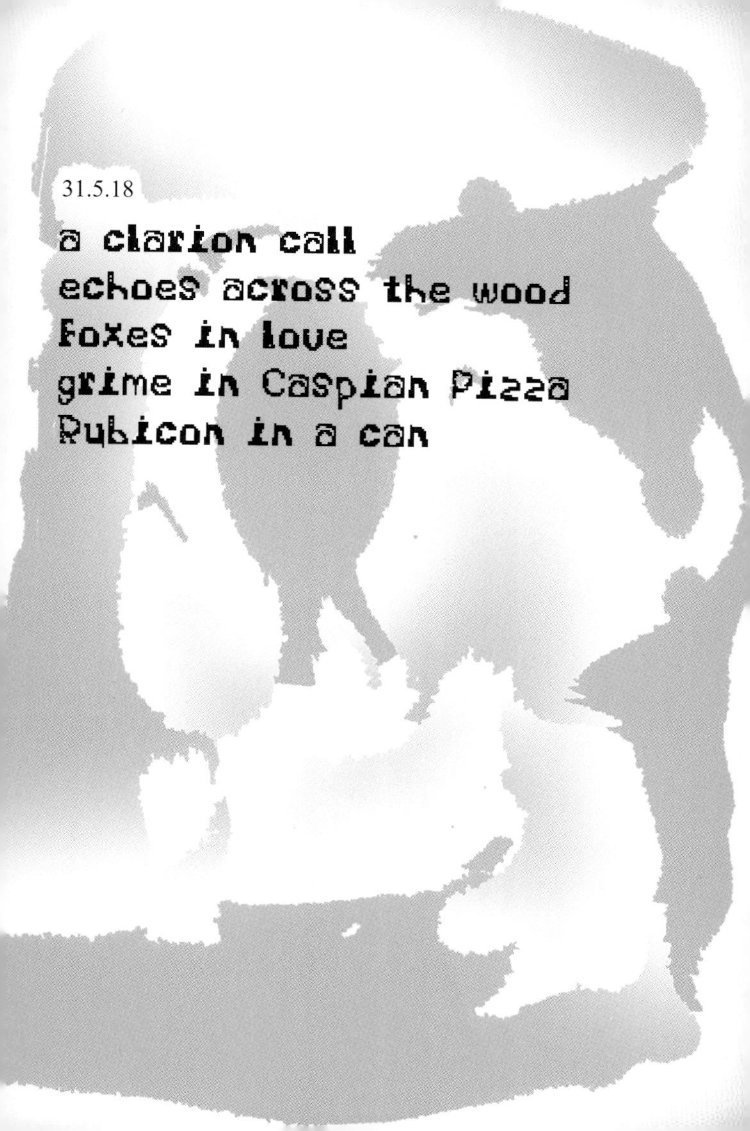

31.5.18

a clarion call
echoes across the wood
foxes in love
grime in Caspian Pizza
Rubicon in a can

24.6.18

dull half moon
cutting shapes in the lawn
after the easy match
she takes off her stilettos
and carries them

2.6.18

a nest of sparrows
over the patio door
morse code
punching through plasterboard
mineral wool on skin

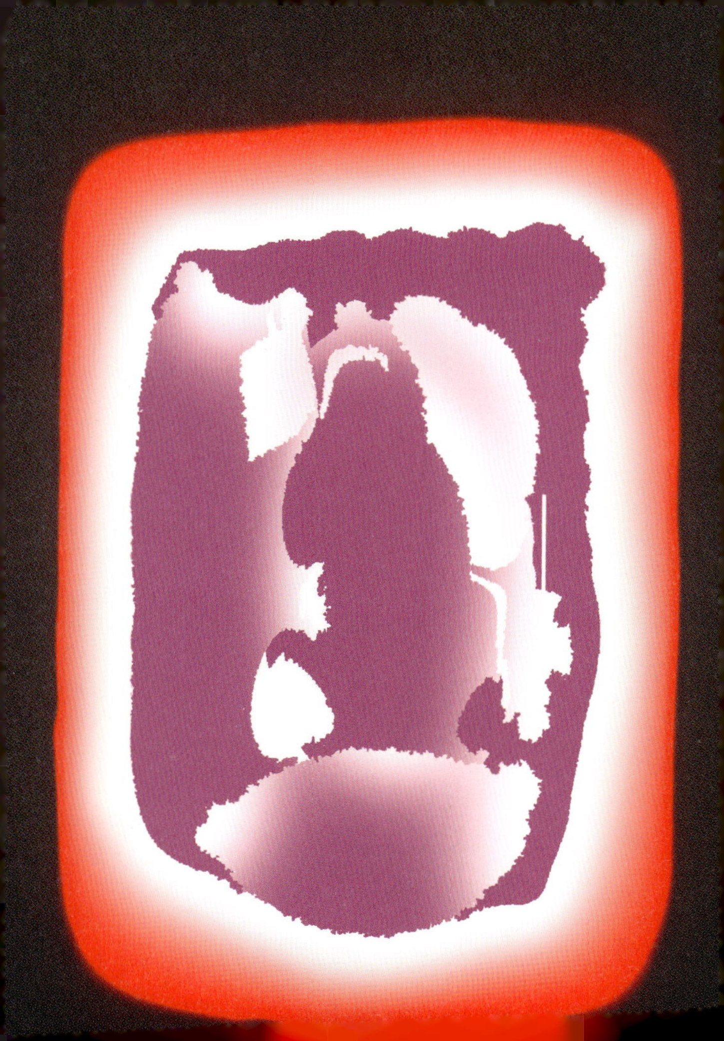

17.7.18

walking on my phone
singing Sufjan
we're all gonna die
a bag of pick n mix
that's just torpedoes

16.7.18

beautiful people
and the great unwashed
la passeggiata
scrubbing blood stains
out of my Margielas

12.7.18

canal pacing
tired mechanics trying
to start the old motor
the curator installs
a defibrillator

26.7.18

eating alfresco
more salad than bacon
in the sandwich shop
glamorous ladies
of wrestling pile up

17.7.18

so beautiful
yet so toxic
but then sago
the starter gun
twitching her reflexes

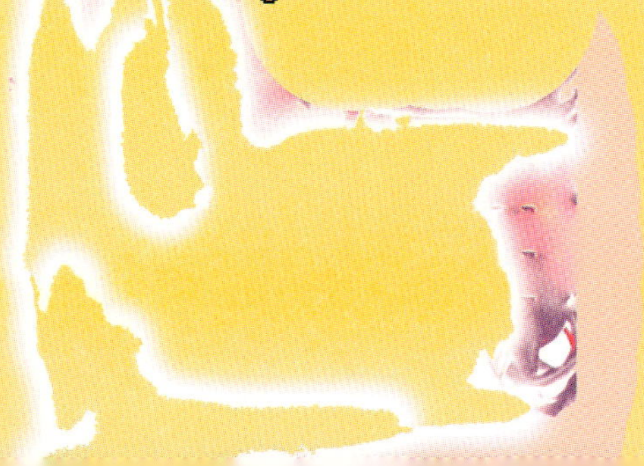

26.7.18

bent at the middle
the mushroom picker
consults his book
under a blood moon
his good queer eye

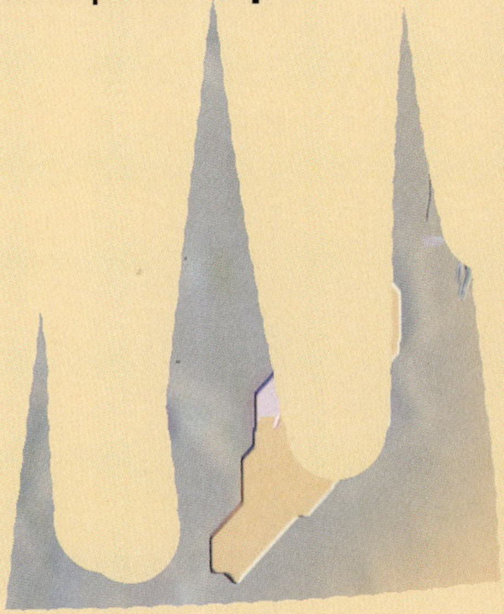

27.7.18

too hot to sleep
the convenience store
fills with chatter
a bright new cap
for H.P's shattered canine

26.7.18

painted over
by the artist in residence
sweet love and romance
throbbing flesh scraping off
the artex in the hallway

28.7.18

far away rain
itching at the edge
of this blooming insect bite
a daylily bent low
by its own weight

27.7.18

our love protests
against all the hate
a gathering storm
they pull the long curtain
slowly across the room

10.8.18

feeling travel sick
on the way to the seaside
a bag of boiled sweets
the stone hurtling towards
this armed soldier's skull

29.7.18

the aftermath
of the teenage house party
cursed gastropod mollusc
do fries go
with that shake?

10.8.18

soaking in the bath
an elk horn fern on cork
opposite tillandsia
his shrink to fit jeans
tight round his thighs

9.8.18

the view from above
throwing one's self out
into the ether
Gwendoline recoils
from the unexpected flash

14.8.18

bucketing water
into a sandcastle moat
the red streaked sky
waiting for the download
stuck at 6

14.8.18

remembering
grandma's jugged hare
white heather
butt cheeks peeping out
of her frayed denim shorts

25.8.18

stopping to gaze
at flags in the border
the smell of bacon
washed so softly
by the Cornish surf

15.8.18

a cream tea for two
in the train station cafe
the silence of wasps
high above the motorway
feeling earthquakes

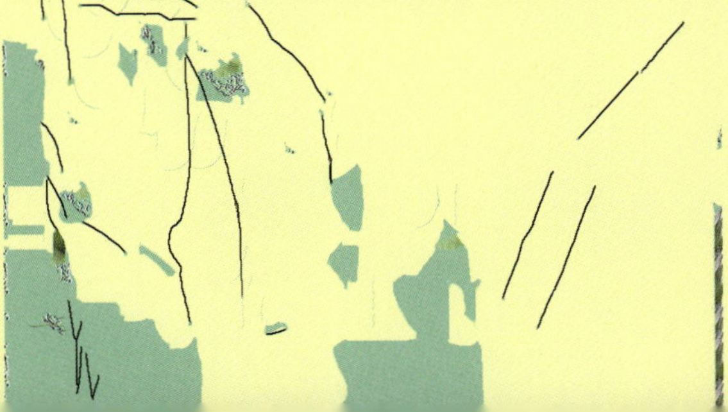

27.8.18

one hundred trees
how small this blister
on my thumb
lines of sediment stacked
and washed by millennia

27.8.18

talking to people
eating food put out
in the same place everyday
stepping stones
from one bank to another

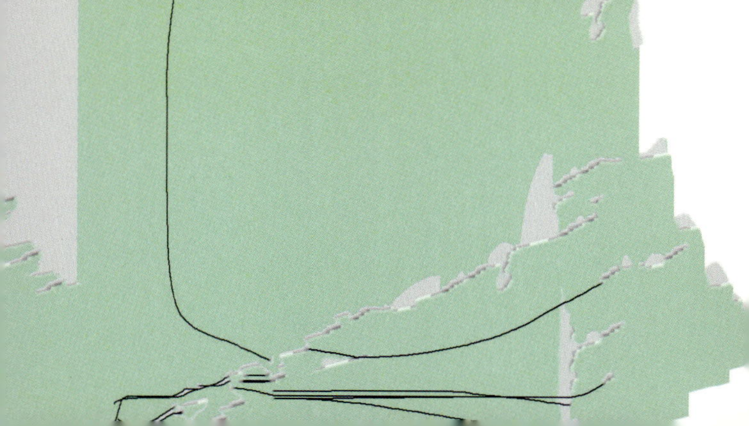

31.8.18

reasserting
raise boys and girls
the same way
real wages fall despite
low unemployment

28.8.18

jangling coins
in my jacket pocket
the busker's dog
spreading public art
to infect the world

1.9.18

new socks slipping inside
my Alexander Wangs
it's the small things
that ensure your life
stays in flux

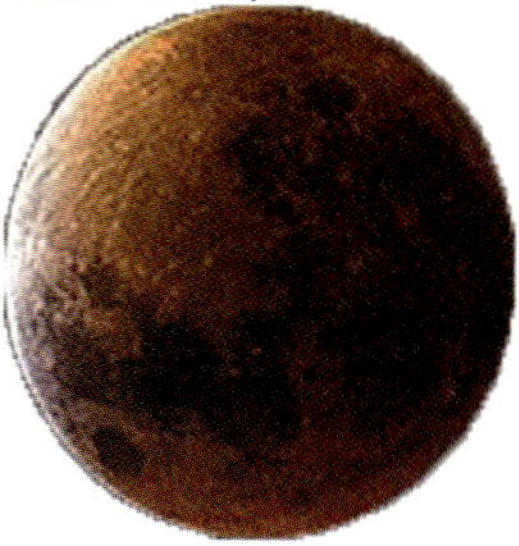

1.9.18

autumn begins
you are a victim
of the rules you live by
new socks slipping inside
my Alexander Wangs

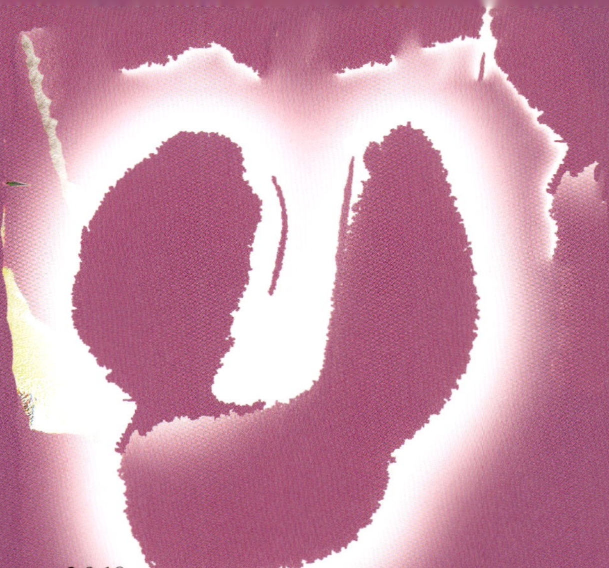

2.9.18

sugar rush
the realisation that dates
come from date palms
the doctor breaks fast
with a mint imperial

7.9.18

2000 AD
minimal technology
for reading on the beach
law as artefact
cows as agents of change

7.9.18

autumn chill
grandma's electric blanket
trips the main fuse
in Wickes weighing up
self levelling compounds

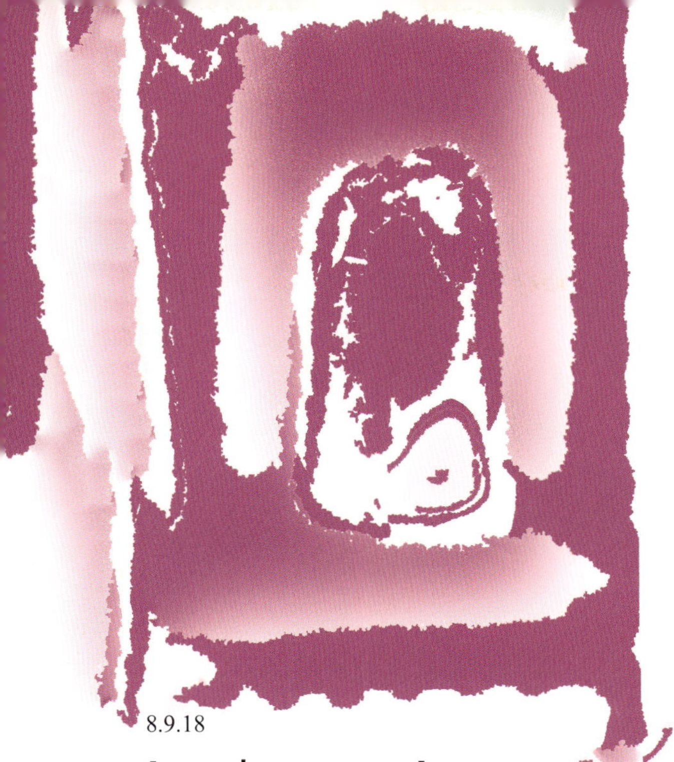

8.9.18

turnip or not
a Cornish pasty
to lift the spirits
covering our stains
on the concrete floor

13.9.18

copy then change but fail
proofing Wikipedia
without knowing why
She searches the shelves
For non GM soya

9.9.18

invaders not refugees
inverting intentions with
the power of a spray can
a song by The Prodigy
repeating in my head

21.9.18 (after Kobayashi Issa 1803)

autumn wind
Wei and Fang rejoice
with two leaves of radish
the electric hoist throbs
as it takes the load

19.10.18

broken beats
two moths trapped
in a lampshade
squarepusher's bass line
improvs my intestines

26.9.18

teenagers fumble
under a canal bridge
lips and drips
the pain and shame
as the ball rolls over the line

26.9.18

lips and drips
the engineer's wait
for tickets to Strictly
the lifts in dad's shoes
are a painful mistake

26.9.18

the electric hoist throbs
as it takes the load
come my selector
the dance floor chants
REWIND

6.10.18

red leaves and coins
in the Neptune Fountain
chattering crowds
the gravitational pull
of an unknown planet

27.9.18

a trillion spores
landing on your skin
eating alfresco
the fire marshall
takes a roll call

7.10.18

buying a paper
the Autumn dew finds
the hole in my shoe
two male moose
loitering by the stream

7.10.18

meteor shower
he pulls the blanket closer
around her shoulders
glistening lube all over
the block and tackle

9.10.18

reading a book
he spills porridge down his tie
chrysanthemums
a rainbow in the puddle
at the petrol station

10.10.18

walking the high wire
across the school yard
a crack in the tarmac
pouring the milk
whisking the egg

9.10.18

the claustrophobia
of his MRI scan
clearing skies
Mike buys his daughter
a first class degree

10.10.18

magpies sift
the bookshop's gutters
two for joy
the monk applies gold leaf
to the marginalia

10.10.18

unexpectedly breathing
lemon sherbet refresher
the crescent moon
a bar crawl with theatrics
and sweet poetry

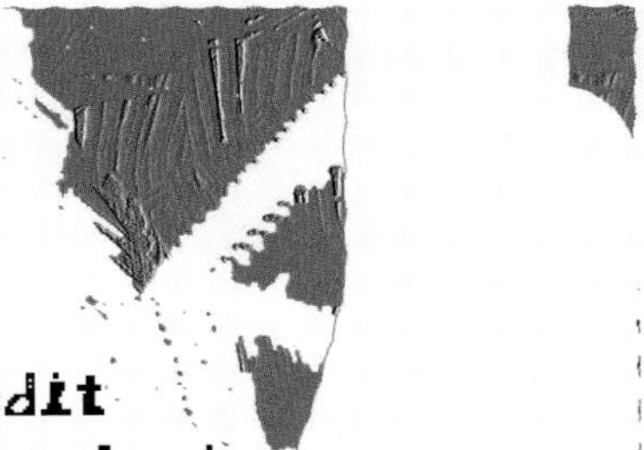

12.10.18

universal credit
an equation employing
coercive technique
she bangs her head on the wall
until she gets her phone back

15.10.18

cold Autumn rain
the smell of chocolate
along birdcage walk
Sylvester makes up
with Tweety Pie

14.10.18

super humans
closing the elite spermbank
due to lack of demand
a sign on the wall
that says No Petting'

14.10.18

tired but happy
the whole night reading
cover to cover
hiding my new passport
in the box under my bed

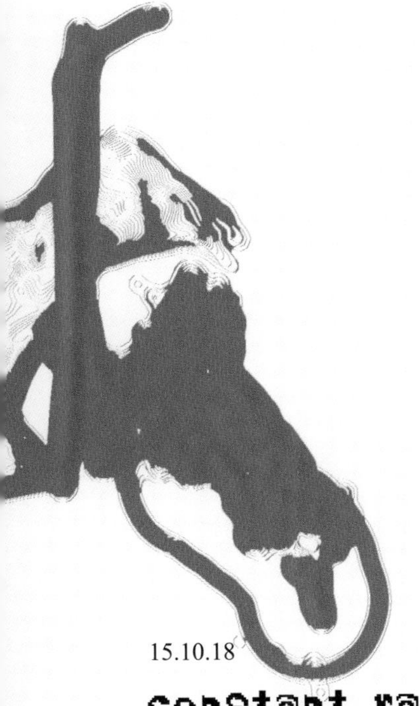

15.10.18

constant rain
next door's cat
on our sofa
in New Babylon
everything is possible

17.10.18

shorter days
the way her toes curl
when he kisses her
40 million kurds
spread around the globe

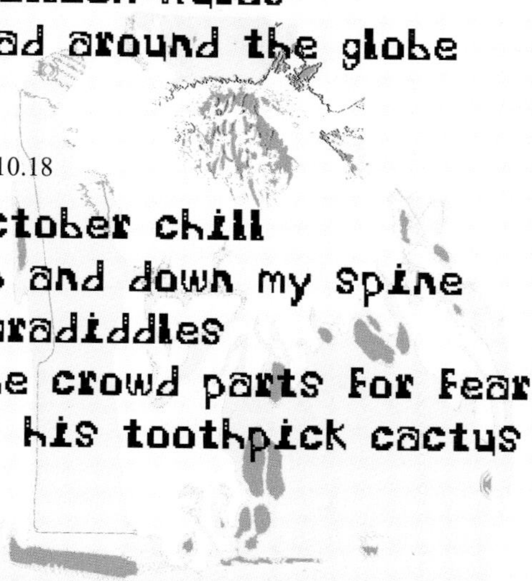

16.10.18

October chill
up and down my spine
paradiddles
the crowd parts for fear
of his toothpick cactus

21.10.18

one kind of luck
or another
crows in a tree
a straight line between
Casablanca and Cadiz

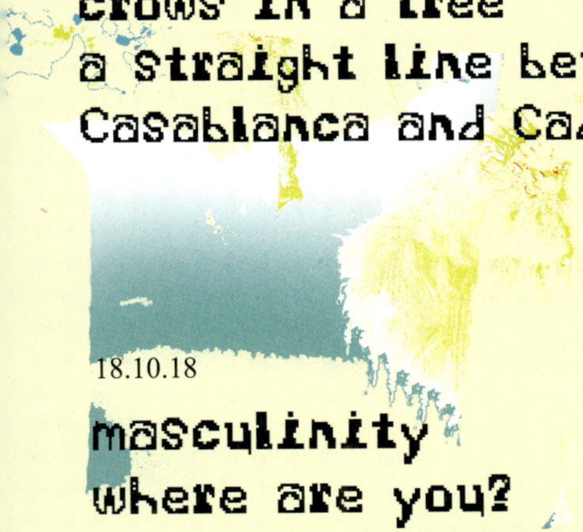

18.10.18

masculinity
where are you?
his pride in knowing
the le and the la
of everything

23.10.18

she thinks that she's
playing with the cat
fish heads and milk
a torture squad
from Saudi Arabi

22.10.18

a border
for a border
a lie for a lie
the taste of her
cherry lip balm

25.10.18

parliament
I search for a few words
to describe the sky
not breathing but fueling
the towerblock's fury

1.11.18

kicking up leaves
I begin to forget
the art gallery
babygod critics
tweeting a shitstorm

30.10.18

a moth egg laid
in the influorescence
of an aged yucca
if you find the Buddha
kill the Buddha

28.10.18

land to land
seaweed trailing
from a turtle's back
watching spaceship Earth
from the surface of the Moon

4.11.18

three chords struck
a Fatsia, red acer
and arundo donax
the eight fingered butcher
takes his turn on the decks

4.11.18

going through dad's stuff
dust and memories
in a cardboard box
Nina Simone and Vanley
on desert island discs

8.11.18

midterm returns
scrambled or fried
the curate's egg
unwrapping a slice
of my birthday cake

7.11.18

feelings are facts
a funeral gang marching
through the market in Rabat
she stirs sugar
into a glass of mint tea

10.11.18

choose
your critics carefully
a watery sun
Wyclef crafts a song
for Destiny's Child

19.11.18

child poverty
is a social calamity
a cold wind blowing
through homes and pensions
the banality of evil

11.11.18

gathering clouds
but for a brain scan
I'd be there with you
using my ESP
to test their USP

20.11.18

closing my eyes
I listen to the pictures
grandad's wireless
slow maggots in the fridge
at the back of the garage

23.11.18

thoughts are metallic
and melt in water
amniorrhexis
the car radio plays
'Sailing' by Rod Stewart

23.11.18

10,000 more people
are homeless
than this time last year
a socially engaged
builder's hoarding

28.11.18

security light
the cat from nowhere
pays court again
the superhero code
of Serena's red sash

27.11.18

zygomorphic flowers
the politician denies
the will of her leader
a worker bee
in love with a drone

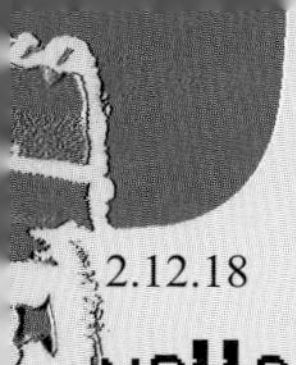

2.12.18

yellow jackets
the justice of sullying
the arc de triomphe
flying under no flag
a bald faced hornet

28.11.18

there was a wall
Ursula dreams the first line
of a feminist novel
held tight in my right
the left hand of darkness

28.11.18

the harmony
of intertwining strings
a thousand kites
flying from BHX
to Johannesburg

5.12.18

perm any two from three
crabapple wild cherry
rowan
I want to break his face
for touching her hair

4.12.18

leaves on fire
the morning garden defrost
at the House of Commons
cardboard boxes
under a railway bridge

9.12.18

there's a stray black cat
in a wigwam tent
down our street
Haudenosaunee women
inspire the suffragettes

9.12.18

early morning fog
you're never alone she says
with a full english
Captain Hook pushes the blade
deep into Peter's back

14.12.18

pushing his dreams
through a steel squeeze wringer
sleet in the wind
testing out a condom
for the very first time

10.12.18

charismatic fervour
I write a letter
to the Corinthians
the word for woman
is not the same as wife
[redacted]

17.12.18

grassland birds
and native grasses
buffalo soldiers
calling out racism
on football terraces

16.12.18

vapour wave
Putin drops Yung Lean
and the crowd goes wild
sad boys in the corner
sip Arizona Iced Tea

19.12.18

the difference
between pee and double u
lipstick and gloss
a self inflicted wound
infused with dark ink

18.12.18

the curve of her cheek
caught in the moonlight
lightly falling snow
shoplifting for Xmas
and some badly needed love

21.12.18

Bashō follows me
across a cold wet Digbeth
Genie Printing chop cards
the Wing Chun master
wins with simplicity

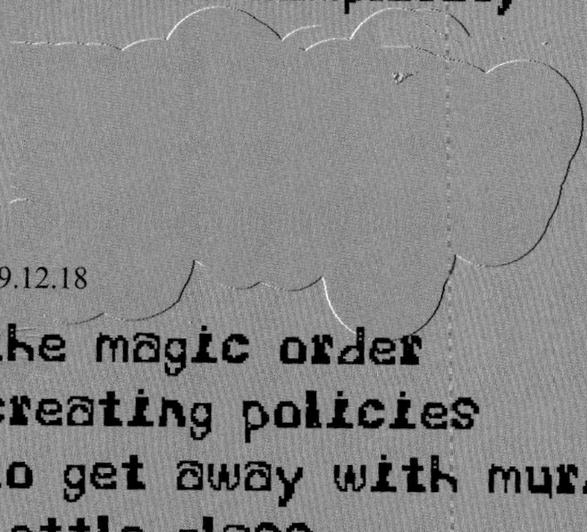

19.12.18

the magic order
creating policies
to get away with murder
bottle glass
glass bottle

26.12.18

tilting at wind farms
I remember a time
when cash registers rang
Japan withdraws the hook
through bloody oily water

22.12.18

19 years in jail
2 kills a socialite
from the West Midlands
a woman a daughter
a sister a friend

28.12.18

almost kickoff
the burger van workers
start to clear down
the insult explodes Al's mind
smashing the chip shop window

27.12.18

a Boxing Day drink
on the way to the football
strangely quiet streets
Rut Blees Luxemburg
captures the tower block

29.12.18

movement of freedom
people in little dinghies
sailing across the channel
her radio dial
sticks on white noise

28.12.18

after four husbands
Mrs Wilson turns to church
the solemn silence
of wilting chrysanthemums
betwixtmas fatigue

1.1.19

on the edge
of 2019
at the old people's home
you do the hokey cokey
and you turn around

30.12.18

reconnection policies
giving homeless people
tickets to nowhere
one way or another
I'm gonna find you

2.1.19

tired of waiting
for the green man
we levitate
switching to soy and lentils
to give the cows a rest

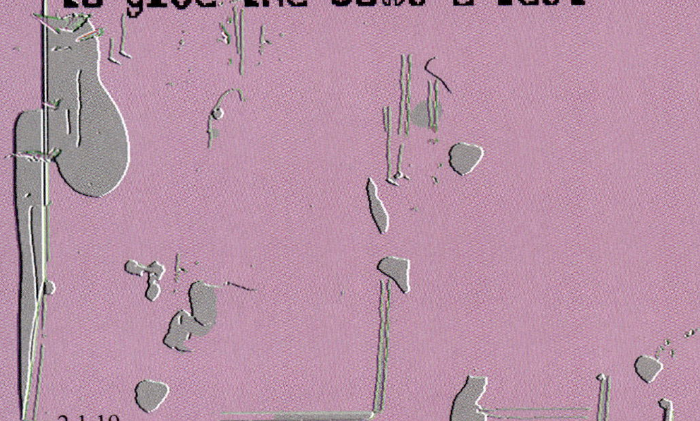

2.1.19

a polar bear
with fishes on its head
howling wind
Eno gets the edit down
and plays it to the boys

9.1.19

evening cool
a fiddle that came apart
in the heat
sweat evaporating
through their string vests

12.1.19

grown so thin
on love and barley
howling in the bath
you may be slowly dying
but I shall go on living

11.1.19

becoming human
seven nights of sex and food
cyborgs and zombies
taking turns round the table
to say who we are

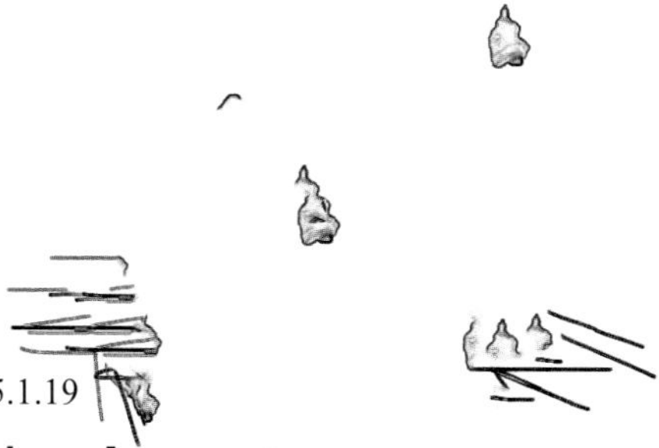

15.1.19

#iamhere
they simply defend those
who are being attacked
a body swerve from
negative to positive

20.1.19

cold to the bone
I take the weight off my feet
two bags of shopping
a hollow digital voice
tells me where to go

17.1.19

the mould
on an English walnut
can kill you
mmm, the perfect girl
living in the perfect world

16.1.19

all through the town
we lean into the wind
gloves and hats
2kg of goat
on the bloody scales

23.1.19

bald for years
I run my wet hands
through my hair
the mangled lorry tyre
on the verge of the M6

21.1.19

super blood wolf moon
we synchronise our phones
to wake us up at six
the cold seeps through
dad's sheepskin coat

28.1.19

still holding a torch
for an old flame
Europe endless
after the horses
we'll muck out the goats

26.1.19

flashes of light
from the peacocks tail
so many tears
all these moments
will be lost in data centers

4.2.19

we talk about the
North Korea nuclear pledge
thickening snow
polished worktops
and shiny mopped floors

3.2.19

even though
I do not need to carry it
my driving licence
a provisional stab
at a ship shape government

10.2.19

grit in my eyes
they say there's a formula
for naming storms
our baby girl writes
her first critical essay

5.2.19

a stitch in time
everyone decides to
revoke article 50
King Harold pulls out
the arrow from his eye

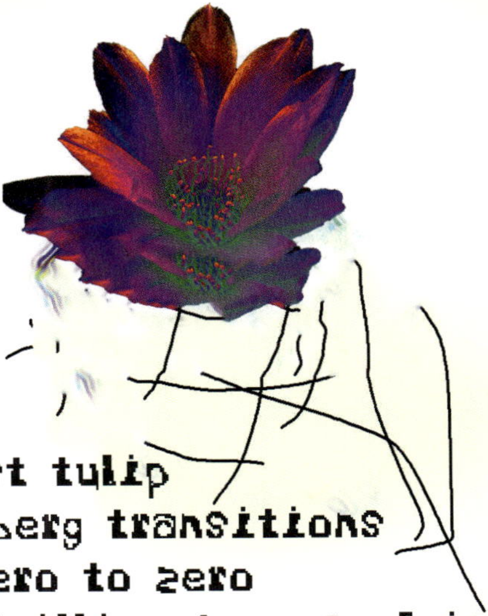

12.2.19

the last tulip
Zuckerberg transitions
from hero to zero
three trillion tonnes of ice
lost since 1992

12.2.19

swept aside
all us old ones
that have been loyal
what went out with the tide
rides back on a wave

16.2.19

pussy willow
I leave my demons
with the cattle
Spike and Buffy's chemistry
turns necro sexual

12.2.19 (after #christopherkirubi)

grinding away
short cycle dopamine hits
of receiving dick pics
it's such a jolly
holiday with Mary

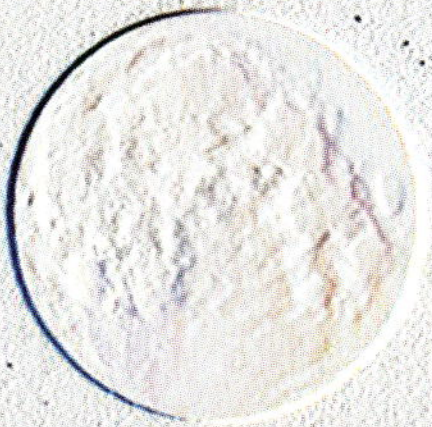

17.2.19

pink blossom on Mars
my battery is low
and it's getting dark
a faint glow
over Sizewell B

19.2.19

Frying tonight
cats gather behind
the fish and chip shop
Bob and Paul compare
conditions of the heart

19.2.19

I follow the rules
until I go against them all
Helen Frankenthaler
Chardonnay's origins
revealed by its DNA

28.2.19

I'd almost forgotten
what your eyes looked like
piss holes in the snow
plaster flowers captured
in bright sunlight

21.2.19

small hot dog
jumbo hot dog
bacon cob
mixing muck and straw
with our bare hands

20.2.19

a new moon
in our solar system
sand in my shoes
rubbing the rough bits
as well as the smooth

28.2.19

chilled to the bone
we make love
in our ankle socks
I take the call during
my keynote lecture

28.2.19

I miss you
I fancy you
I wish I was touching you
Tracey has a gin
served in a mug

2.3.19

sunshine and showers
we're going to take this
to the next level
Freya makes atmospheric
changes to the lighting

1.3.19

you're a big man
in bad shape
behave yourself
quadrophonic sound
and socks on pink underlay

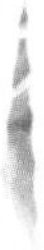

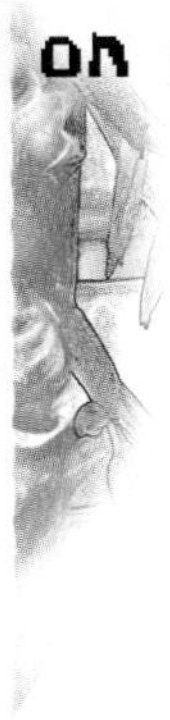

2.3.19

it's a funny thing
the half moon
scrolling Baburnama
with confidence she tells me
that tulips are from Turkey

2.3.19

a pint of bitter
in a straight glass
embedded assumptions
encoded in expecting
this seamless conformity

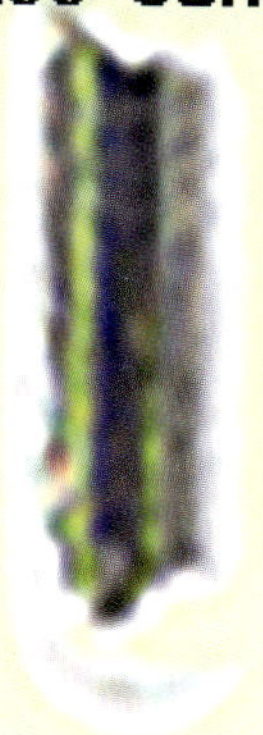

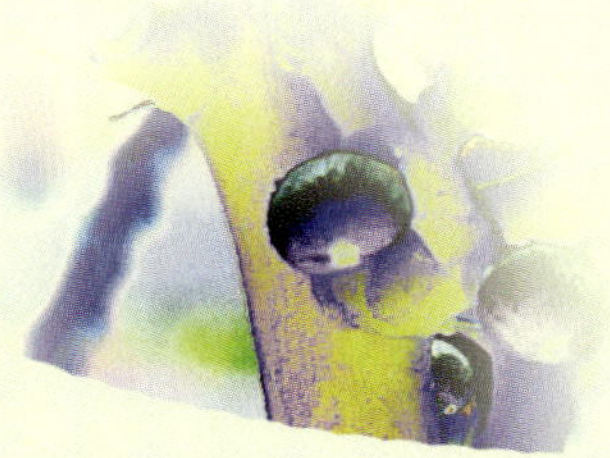

2.3.19

creation myths
the early Spring triggers
an explosion of tulips
changes in the body
of our low estate

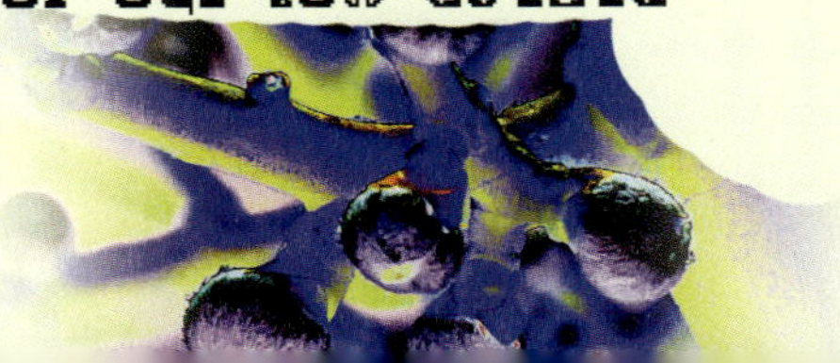

2.3.19

I've got a feeling
we aren't going to get
a fee for this job
she turns back smiling
and gives me a wave

2.3.19

good evening Gavin
I see my colleague tried
to contact you last week
a cuckoo chick
in a dunnock's nest

2.3.19

you know my life
machines, the arcades
oxeye daisies
tripping himself he falls
onto his broken hand

2.3.19

time passes
I carry on looking up
into the sky
Murdoch Priestly and Watt
coated in gilded bronze

13.3.19

a face in the crowd
the low sun and a pigeon
slowly cross the pitch
the Birmingham massive
share an obscure joke

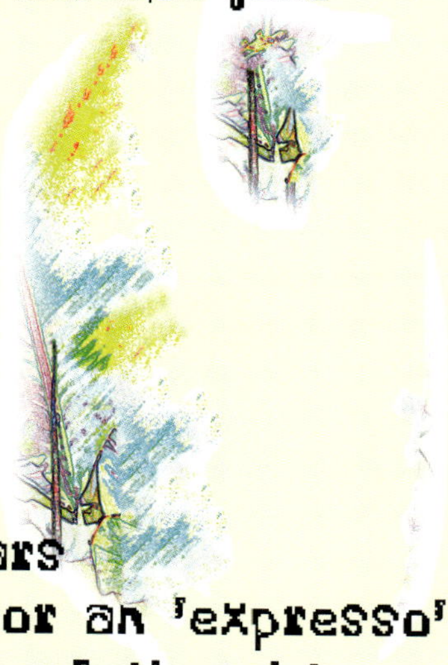

12.3.19

for years
I ask for an 'expresso'
a train of thought
issuing compulsory
purchase orders

13.3.19

walking to the match
a police motorcycle
shoots the traffic lights
reliving the final scene
of The OA Part 1

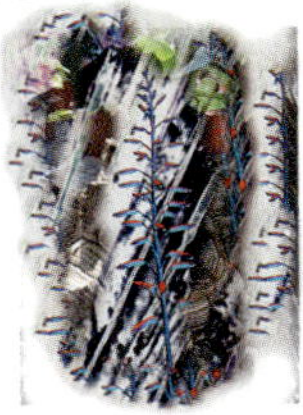

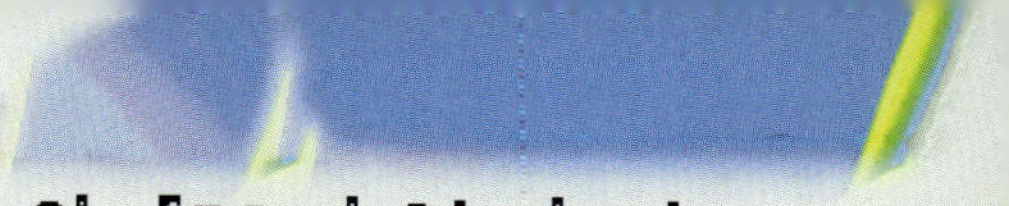

16.3.19

a fresh faced student
tells me all about context
a spring gale blowing
for each marble step
a different colour

27.3.19

at the petting farm
a sheep seems to say
let my people go
her tights shimmer
with the blues and twos

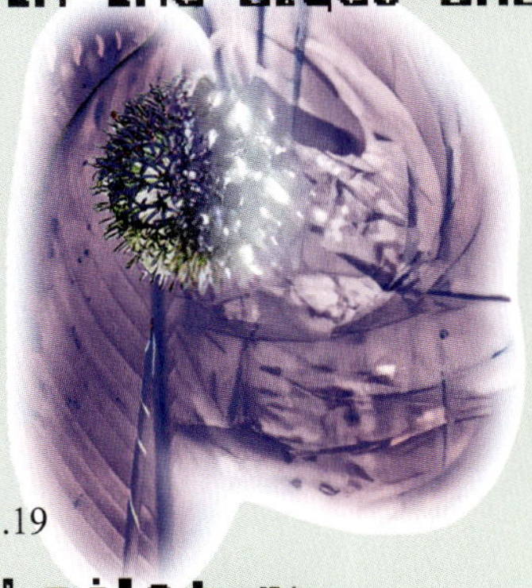

17.3.19

a hailstorm
then bright sunshine
wild crocus
the midlife balance
of births and deaths

29.5.19

my woman she can't
help me with my mind
freezing fog
they searches Kowloon for
extra aphrodisiac

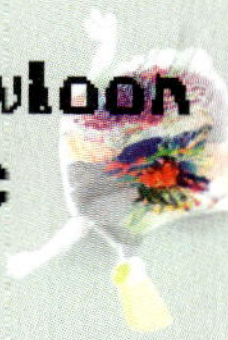

4.5.19

regenerative action
or face extinction
don't fuck with nature
their pelvic muscle's
got a real tight grip

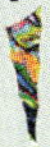

5.4.19

a fast flowing stream
in the shade of a willow
ducks and drakes
my phone sells my data
to the highest bidder

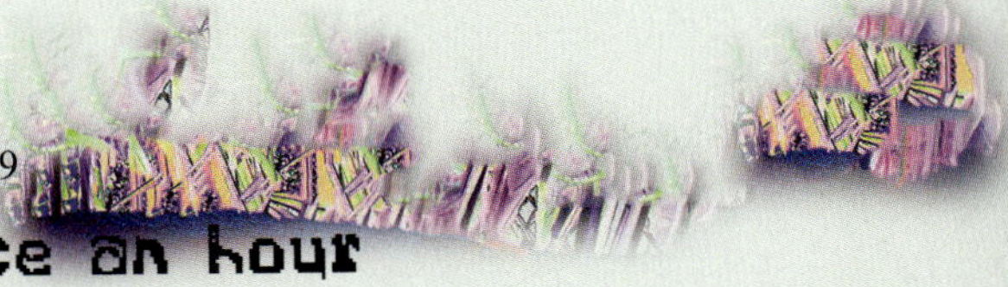

29.5.19

once an hour
the restaurant drops
blossom from the ceiling
hashtag mango
hashtag chutney

9.6.19

keeping an eye on
the tornado behind him
he mows the back lawn
Venus and Serena in
the Wimbledon arena

7.6.19

time passes quickly
when I'm with my son
daisies in long grass
John's chucked the chain
really high in the air

15.6.19

people think
that I'm insane
frowning all the time
a shallow channel cut
in the surface of soil

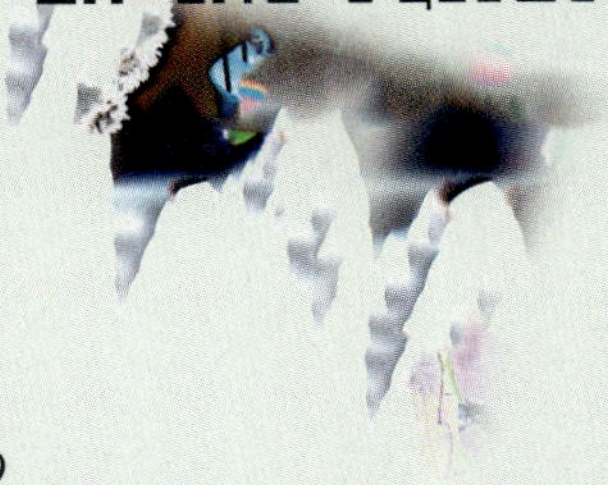

14.6.19

the nervousness
of an edge
planted with love
he smuggles a sharp blade
into the system

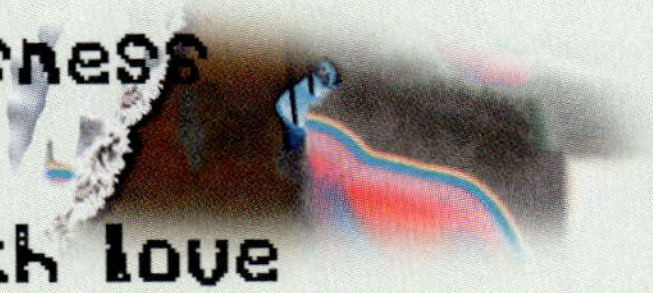

15.6.19

I'll lose my mind
if I don't find something
to pacify
it's only there
trying to fool the public

15.6.19

the last swallow
I think of things but nothing
seems to satisfy
Venom bites another
bad guy's head clean off

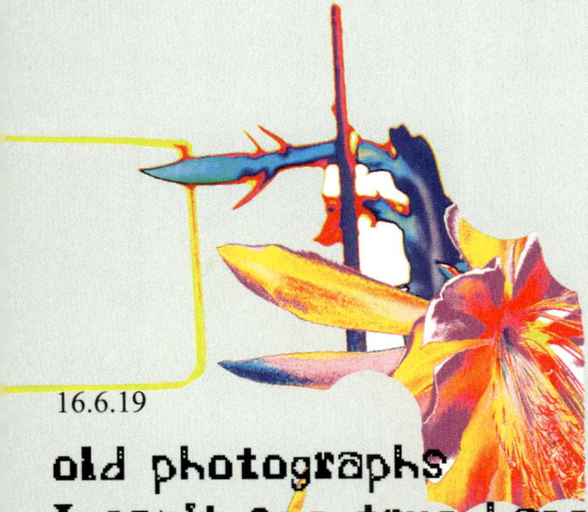

16.6.19

old photographs
I can't see true happiness
I must be blind
on the scales converting
pounds to kilograms

15.6.19

counting daisies
can you help me
occupy my brain?
memorising the views
from Table Mountain

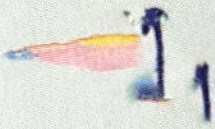

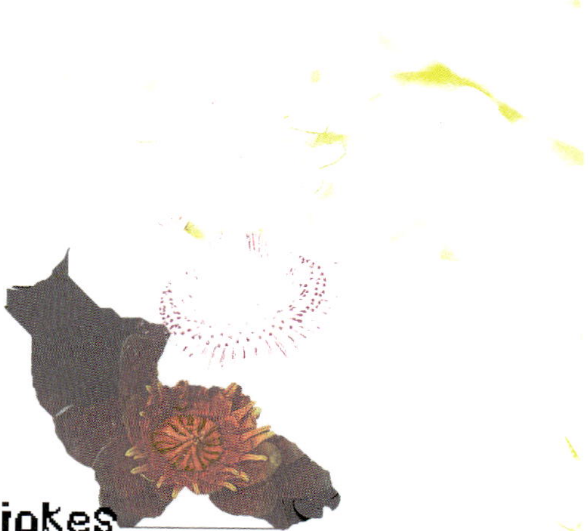

16.6.19

your jokes
I sigh you laugh I cry
blossom in the wind
punching thousands of holes
in sheets of metal

17.6.19

I can't feel happy
love to me is so unreal
dead ash trees
the decomposition
of trade relations

17.6.19

busy workers
standing in trees
pollinating blossom
the zen beekeeper
shakes his head

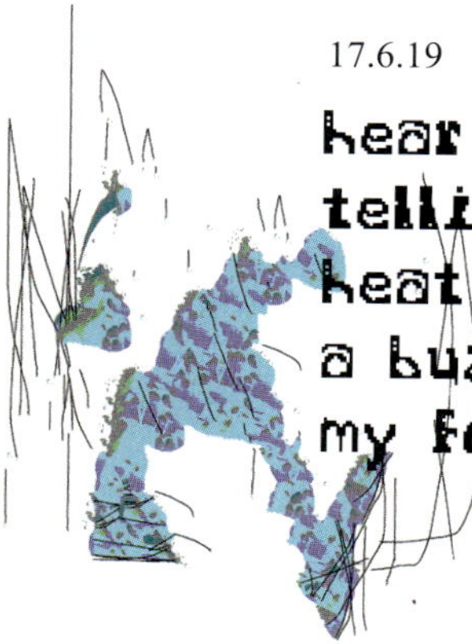

17.6.19

hear these words
telling you of my state
heat and dust
a buzzard intersects
my forward momentum

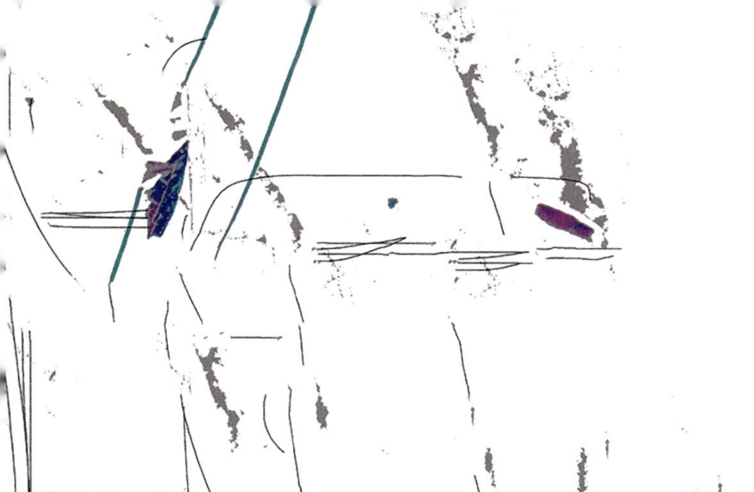

30.6.19

a pipistrelle bat
I'm getting my kicks
out on the floor
chart checking the shade
of my urine flow

17.6.19

I say to you enjoy life
I wish I could
but it's too late
checking the number
of weeks since they bled

6.7.19

folds, tucks and layers
seem to matter more
the older I get
origami and the art
of hospital corners

5.7.19

symbiotic cultures
far away machines
slicing white bread
an aromatic essence
piped in with the Muzak

13.7.19

denied being
a folding screen with
a painting of a mountain
the soft contours
of the small of your back

13.7.19

public assembly
failing to comply
with a condition imposed
we scan the airwaves
for skylarks

6.7.19

summer heat
her one raised eyebrow
shuts him the fuck up
the jack of hearts
with a sleight of hand

18.7.19

people are bewitched
into believing
that time slips away
washing porcelain
from our tired hands

1.8.19

sustainability
so much energy used
growing hair and nails
the nutritionist tells me
to eat more omega three

23.7.19

our prime minister
to whom lying comes
as easily as breathing
ugly vulgar gluttonous
dishonest stupid jejune

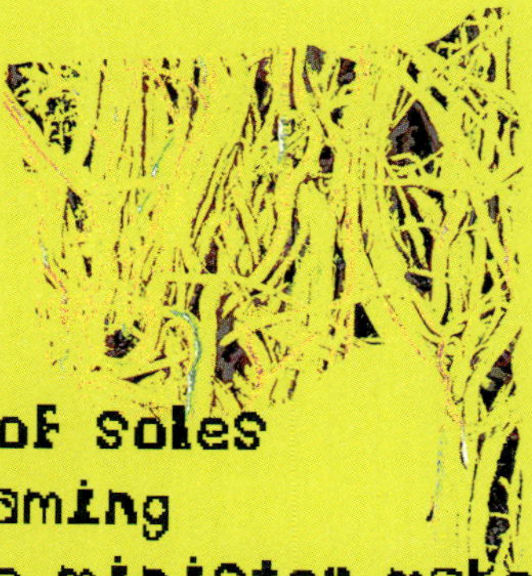

12.8.19

evensong
a panoply of soles
in the gloaming
the culture minister makes
a merciless decision

12.8.19

dawn chorus
a choir of angelfish
and a seahorse
laser beams bouncing
off the park in the sky

14.8.19

we consider it
unfinished until
it's made accessible
a symphony of lifts
and dropped kerbs

14.8.19

revolution
what they gain
is for all of us
notes in the margins
of a little red book

14.8.19

the refrigerator
has social media
capabilities
a macro expert network
of chilled prawns and lettuce

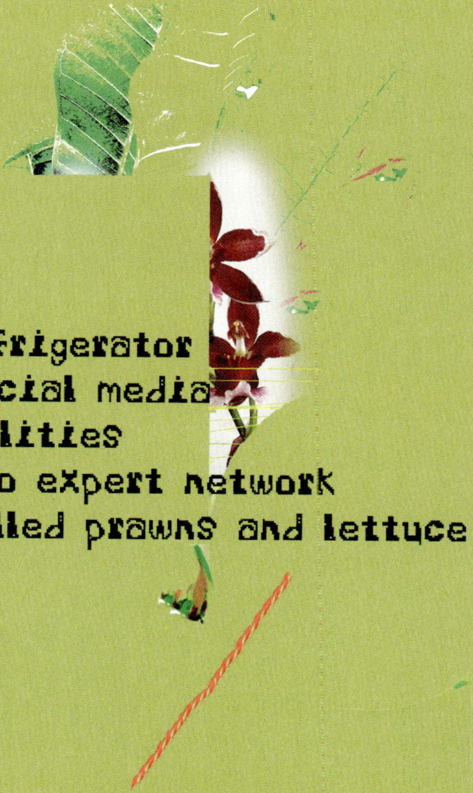

16.8.19

immortality
lipstick palms
and frangipanis
a this and that history
written in wrinkles

14.8.19

pouring rain
someone else's cat
asleep on our bed
trying out positions
on the airport seat

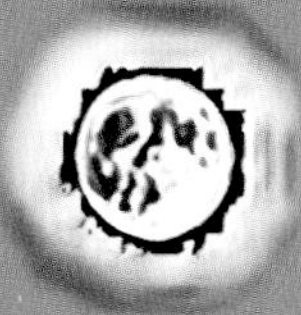

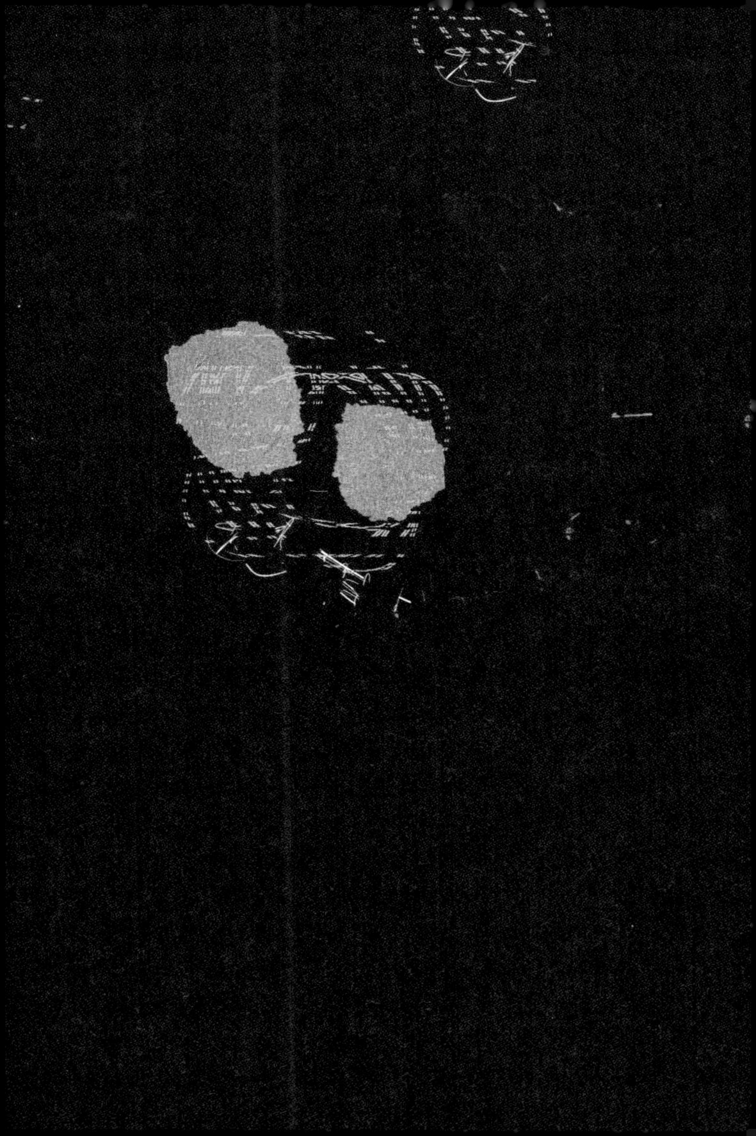

24.8.19

something stirs
deep inside my chest
a laughing dragon
two shades of grey
becoming one

18.8.19

an egg custard
the taste of nutmeg
and coming home
the little black cat
runs between my legs

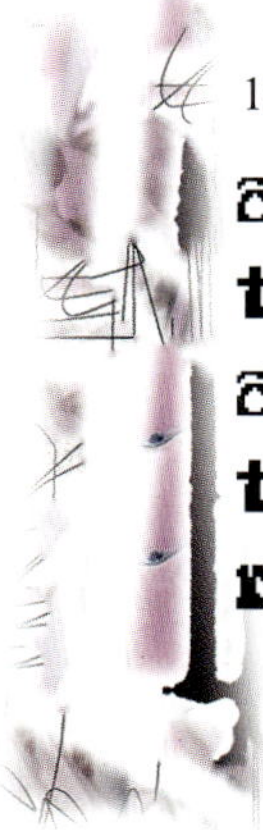

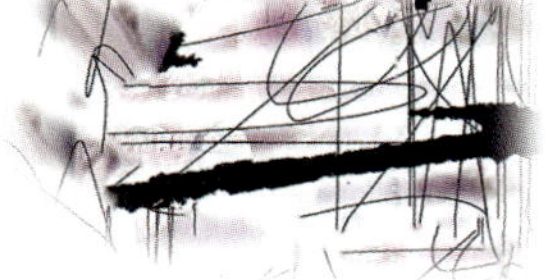

26.8.19

slow motion po po
signs of gentrification
and strategic GBH
tri-nitrate spray keeps me
up on the dance floor

25.8.19

little brother
planning to cut down
the recognition towers
I gradually become
my mother's father

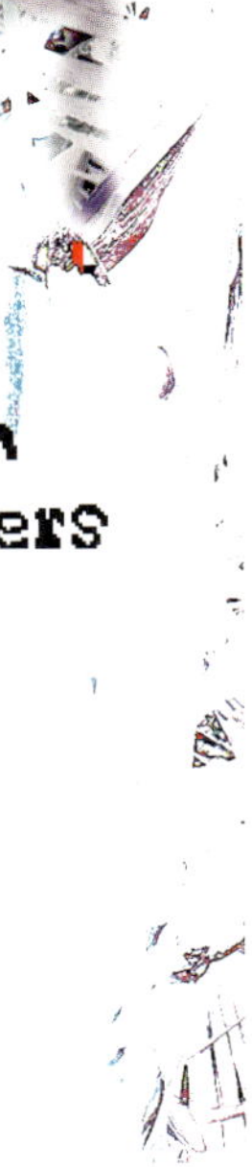

29.8.19

no confidence
a silly little man
doing things badly
his scrumping returns
a bag of sour apples

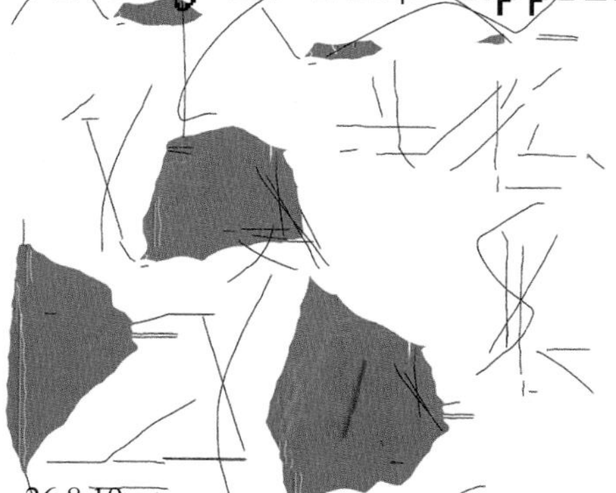

26.8.19

hot and humid
my mother asks again
if she's had her painkillers
carrying a post it note
up to the top floor

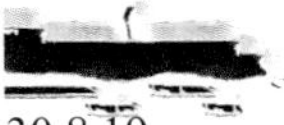

30.8.19

Friday morning
I'm feeling already tired
of the day to come
rubber stolen
from far away

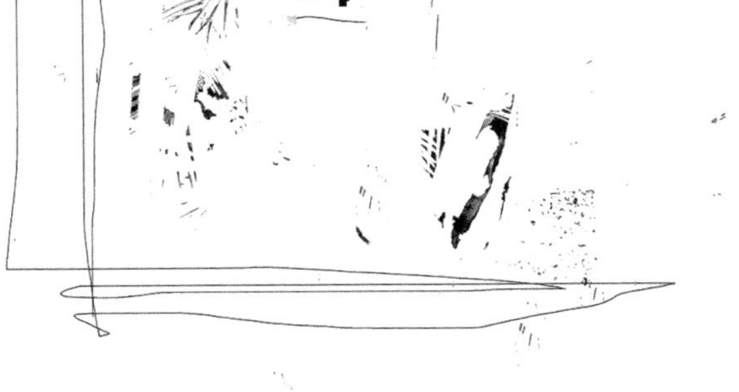

31.8.19

rubber stolen
from far away
a pneumatic drill
cutting right through
my morning mantra

31.8.19

to be led
by a liar is to ask
to be told lies
the farmer tells his pigs
that he loves them

4.9.19

dozing off
in a takeout container
paving slab ridges
hard and damp through
my old sleeping bag

3.9.19

kill all the birds
with all the stones
pre election panic
we listen in vain
for the sound of the dodo

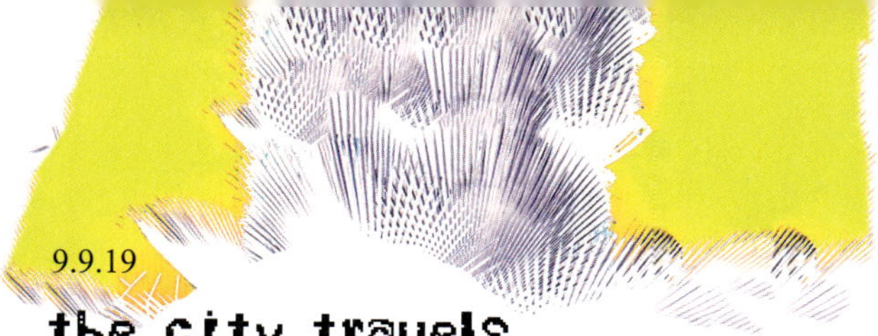

9.9.19

the city travels
on the sweat of workers
smoking mirrors
very gently pulling
Smithson's floating island

7.9.19 (after Pamela Anderson)

undemocracy
this western world
fighting to get more rich
oh Oh OH
sweet love und romance

4.9.19

becoming moths
lovers meet
in Hidalgo Station
a cloak thrown over
a marble column

13.9.19

with words spoken
in public and in private
defend democracy
tongue to tongue
we declare our rights

13.9.19

5 a.m. alarm
I reach out into the day
and find yesterday
the troubles start up again
on the bloody border

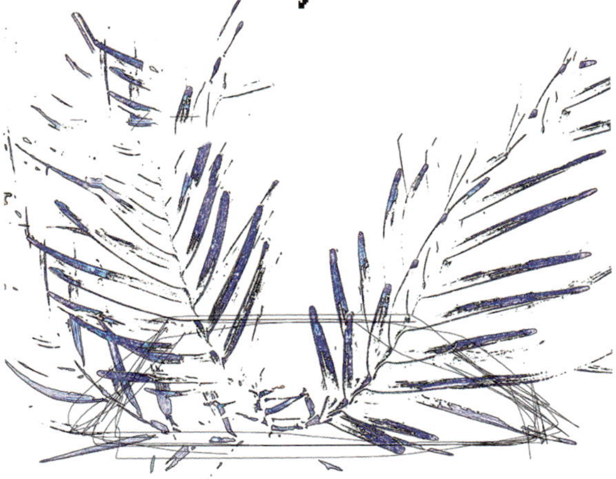

17.9.19

caught free soloing
the inverted ziggurat
domestic homicide
statistics hit
an all time high

16.9.19

footsteps
on the apples
dad's midnight snack
caught free soloing
the inverted ziggurat

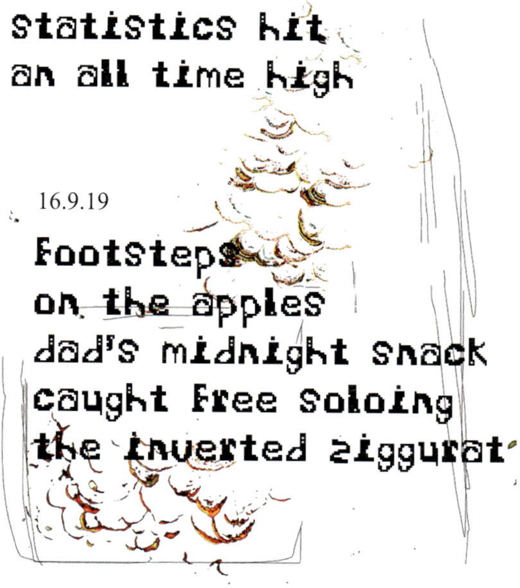

20.9.19

post pollination
luxury communism ends
disaster capitalism
hands that do dishes
can be soft as your face

20.9.19

feeling I'm aboard
a tall ship in a storm
my mother's health
the Belisha beacons
on the way to school

26.9.19

the city moves
on the sweat of workers
smoking mirrors
her bright burning stick
pokes through the !kwe

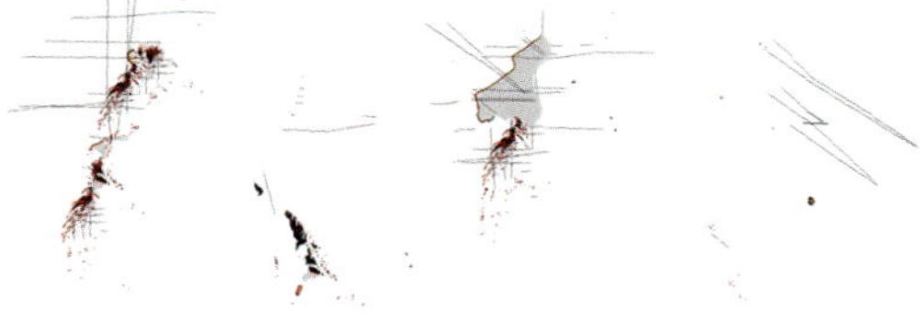

29.9.19

the wait each night
for you to come to me
earth spider
whispering messages
sent by the old gods

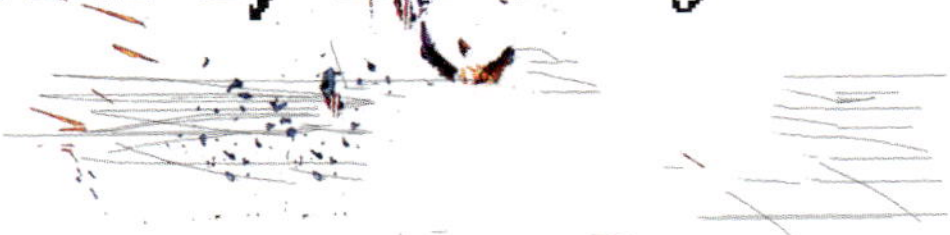

28.9.19

what's that? what's that?
down by the tuna stand
a pork pie hat
Lenny lets go of the girls
coveting the tough guys

15.11.19

crowds gather to watch
the death of Captain Webb
his flailing arms
time passing by
and ever increasing

16.12.19

I have found myself
face down in a pile of chips
but that's Zen for you
the cod's barbule tickles
the struggling octopus

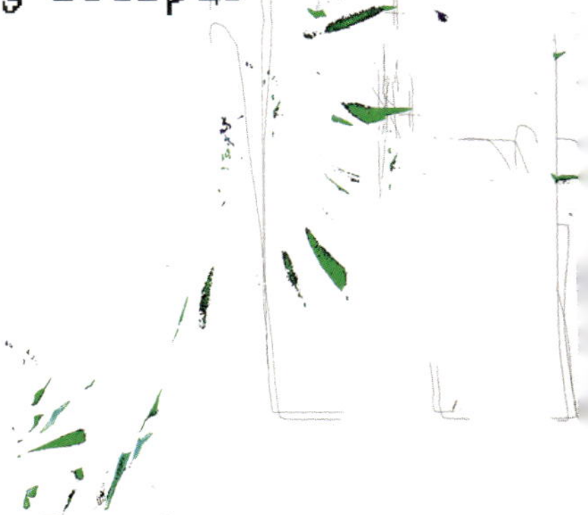

15.12.19

street furniture
don't crush my spirit
with pains and torment
ointment smeared
over a lingering rash

12.1.20

ten seconds
of giving the order
to fire missiles
Eros takes Psyche
to meet his mother

9.1.20

the printmaker
stops by for lunch
ink and hair
drunken calligraphy
with noodles and prawns

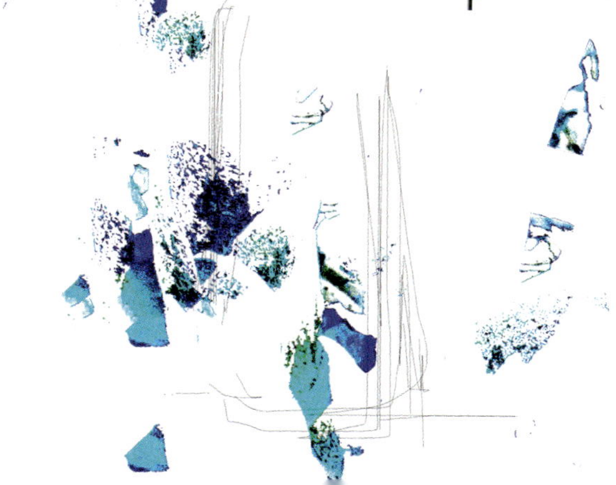

28.1.20

being part of
the dying of the light
snow on the footpath
a very big bruise
from such a little slip

23.1.20

coronavirus
nobody in or out
of the city of Wuhan
the clan lay down
some old skool beats

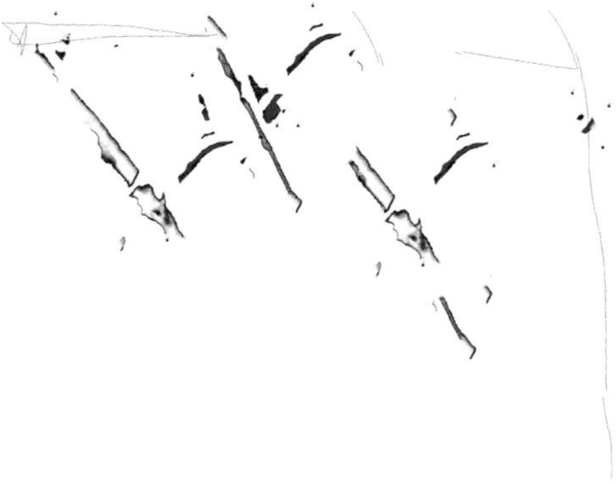

29.1.20

the radish seller
points out the way to me
with Issa's radish
fresh ingredients
from the old market

12.2.20

the ordinary
is extraordinary
illuminated
people start to notice
will.i.am's tell

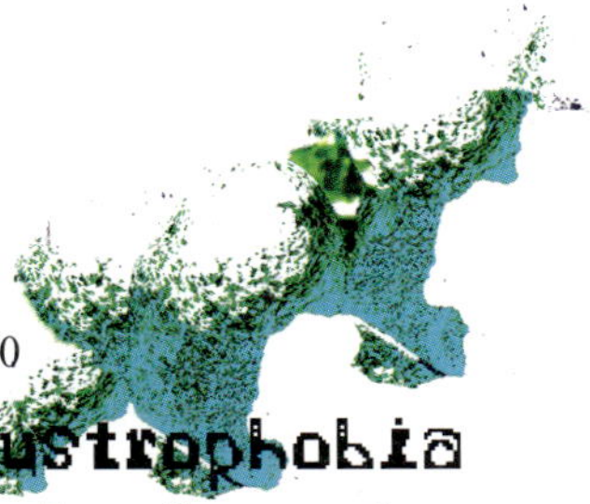

12.2.20

claustrophobia
the barber shaves my head
twice
the museum director
pretends to be impressed

17.2.20

failing health
chewing dried seaweed
my teeth grate on sand
the slow sediment
of lake succession

14.2.20

at the point
where one system
meets another
the gauge changes
and we cross the border

14.2.20

soft sweet darkness
lightness electricity
of your skin
so many memories
still to be made

19.2.20

a real racist
outlining the new
immigration policy
what do points make?
points make prizes

17.2.20

the slow sediment
of lake succession
a spoonful or two
of milk of magnesia
each night before bed

23.2.20

Moon Jae-in
places South Korea
on red alert
holding back a cough
the priest breaks wind

23.2.20

knit one purl one
the fog and the moon
come together
breathlessly we both
whisper I love you

26.2.20

early morning walk
deciphering the chatter
of overhead lines
rising petrol
from belly to mouth

23.2.20 sun down
a loss of sixty eight
million bad debts
he pays for lunch
with his phone

1.3.20

crimson and clover
you cannot teach
an old dog new tricks
scratching at the itch
just out of reach

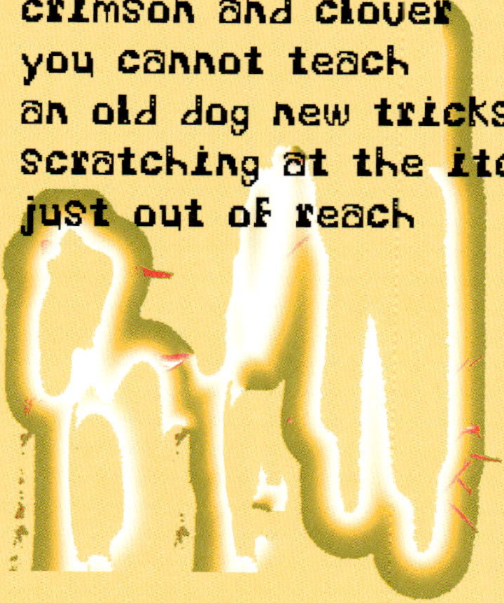

10.3.20

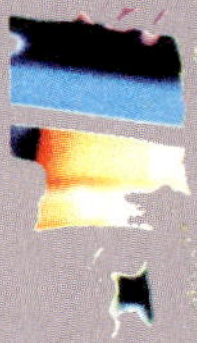

the old pond
becomes young again
tadpoles and froglets
born of the eye's
faint convexity

3.3.20

another ankle
twisted on the cobbles
by the Digbeth bus stops
if you fancy a sit down
there's more room on top

3.3.20

first shave
of the new year
my ears
sucking idly
on a slice of persimmon

10.3.20

her macular
brings visions
of dead children
a dry bottom
but soaking wet knees

10.3.20

born of the eye's
faint convexity
her macular
brings visions
of dead children

19.3.20

edamame beans
she strips them with her teeth
and discards the pods
riding the biggest wave
just for fun

18.3.20

the cold air
against your cheeks
camellia blooms
a rush of blood
to the nether regions

8.4.20

big owl waits
for pink moon
in eucalyptus tree
going nowhere soon
he maintains his quiff

31.3.20

staring at
a Hiroshige print
I become rain
the words be liquid
hidden in the binding

13.4.20

counting props
in a Hiroshige print
night rain at Karasaki
I remember your face
lit by fireflies

10.4.20

listening to
last year's spring playlist
I mow the lawn twice
measuring up to replace
a lost greenhouse fixing

19.4.20

isolation
the same robin song
over and over again
the complex high hat
patterns of trap

18.4.20

social distancing
a man on a fast bike
tells me to fuck off
the flags flapping
outside the British Legion

29.4.20

before breakfast
we fold into each other
poached eggs
the first time we
write poetry together

26.4.20

clapping Tories
when this is over
there will be a reckoning
breathing in empty
football stadiums

16.5.20

holiday season
the stewardess remembers
when she used to fly
for a brief period
she was a terrorist

7.5.20

humid for May
purple passion flowers
against a brick wall
Prince and Spike Lee
cheer on Michael Jordan

2.5.20

on my walk
I find passion flowers
hailstones
prickling up my skin
and messing with my senses

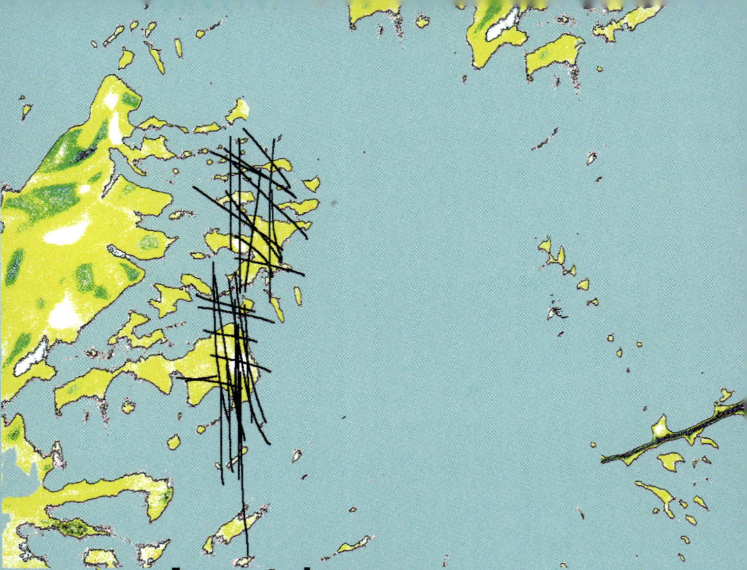

16.5.20 almost home
a field of young barley
talks to my feet
I follow the she cat
wherever she takes me

16.5.20 spring fever
we dance with members
of our own household
as if there is a before
and after life

27.5.20

shall I compare
you to a rose?
ears and hands
Barbara Hepworth
weeps in the garden

23.5.20

I follow the she cat
wherever she takes me
a quick snog
and a fumble
behind the Chinese

30.6.20

local lockdown
the hairdresser perms
her own hair
with enough grease
all the pins click into place

27.5.20

the unkindness of ravens
follows the artist
to the rose garden
petal by petal
we explore self love

4.7.20

edamame konbu
plum leaf and rice ball
this summer rain
she tucks me in
with a loving kiss

30.6.20

deep in lockdown
a clean shirt and tie
each morning
switching back between
heat and ice pack

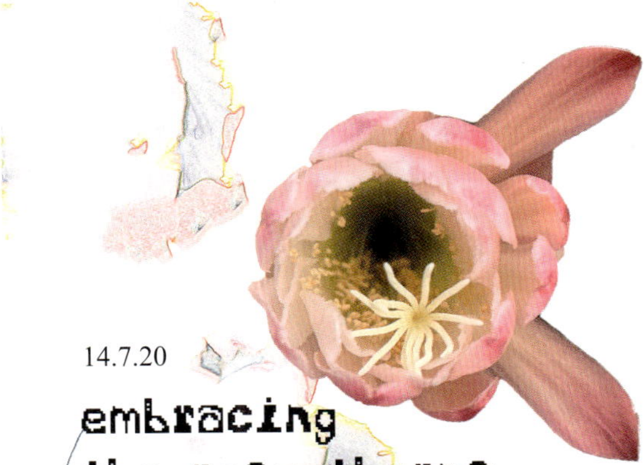

14.7.20

embracing
the rose thorns
and all this life
fresh cat scratches
crisscrossing old

14.7.20

and they say that
space is the final frontier
my toe pokes the sea
deja vu vibration
in an empty pocket

14.7.20

energy release
too much data
ruining the world
dad tries to remember
mum's first name

25.7.20

unconscious bias
populism
fucks people over
the pick n mix section
suspended

24.7.20

blues and whites
the whole afternoon
spent reading clouds
our shared future
after the revolution

15.7.20

another new statue
repeating problems
we want rid of
Uncle never forgets
to salute magpies

17.8.20

the strap
it pinches me
just at the crease
a glance off the toes
towards square leg

27.7.20

slicing off fat
in order to better
share global wealth
Jack Sprat's wife
licks the platter clean

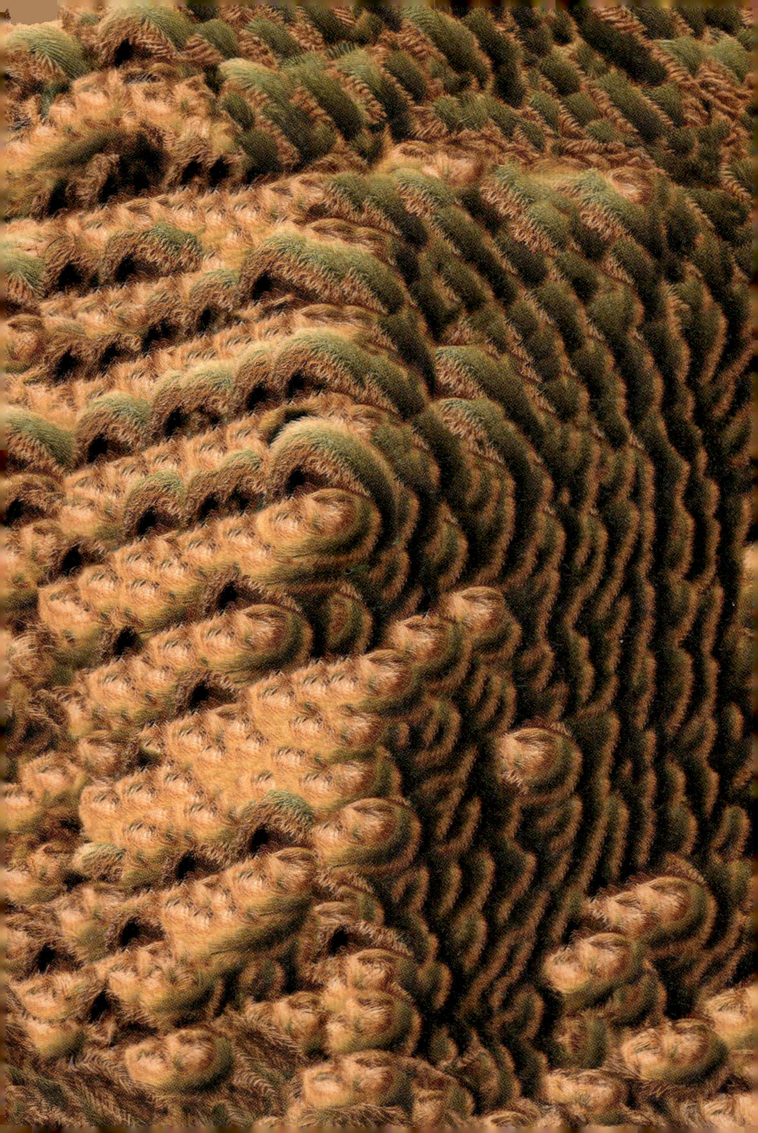

23.8.20

a break in the rain
I soak myself in the light
of the midnight sky
an ad hoc splint
for the fallen protestor

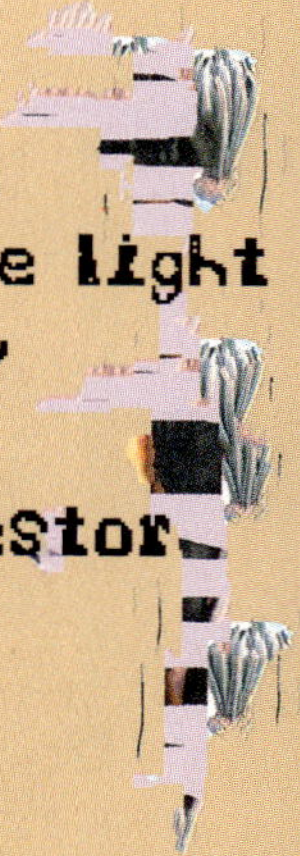

17.8.20

She recites
The Internationale
in 45 seconds
how long does a peaceful
change of power take?

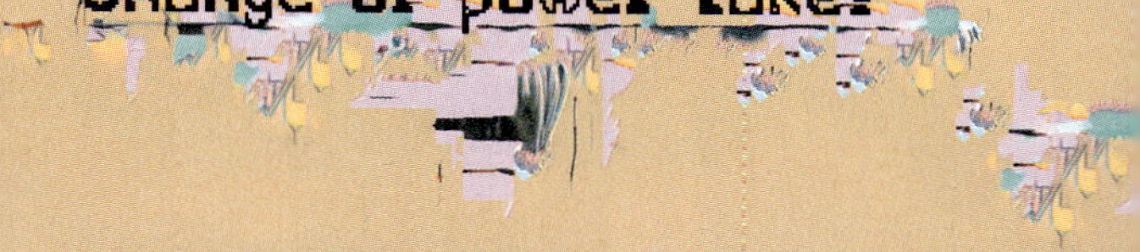

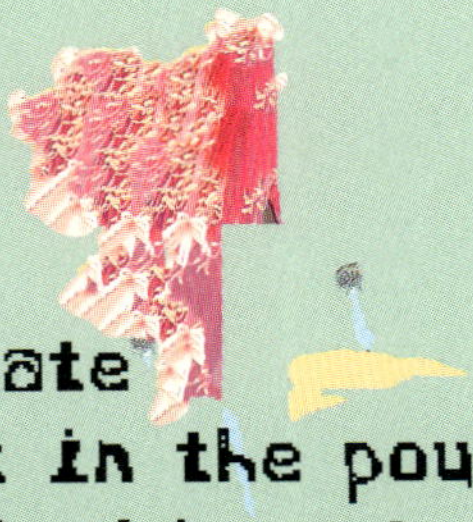

25.8.20

waking late
barefoot in the pouring rain
I drag the bin out
a scar in the spirit world
lasting millennia

24.8.20

no more parties
a million brummies
asleep in their homes
murmurations of starlings
swirl then settle in the trees

29.8.20

the black panther
we all salute the man
and the forever
my wife reminds me
to send back my bowel test

2.9.20

not wild but farmed
the dreams of dead soldiers
move with the wind
a billion insects
transfer pollen

2.9.20

bad algorithm
the minister is forced
to make a u turn
the music goes round and round
and comes out here

9.9.20

I spend the whole night
pulling my thoughts together
vegetable soup
sieving out the bindweed
from the good soil

4.9.20

little onion
sixty one times
around the sun
five pills in the morning
four at night

23.9.20

shopping for nails
the assistant hands me
Great Expectations
the artist bites
the hand that feeds us

9.9.20

born slippy drops
on the kitchen stereo
sunflowers
suddenly the world
feels liveable

25.10.20

two trillion debt
the hum of insects
all over the garden
deleting their messages
once bitten twice shy

25.9.20

we spend the morning
planting up the back border
jellyfish kisses
hundreds of whales
wash up on the shore

5.10.20

at your service
the overwhelming might
of the British state
in the long run it's cheaper
to have all your teeth out

1.10.20

high above
the city's honk and hum
returning geese
me and my mates
climb the cathedral

28.9.20

the last apples
I find an old recipe
for my first chutney
we clean the windows
with newsprint and vinegar

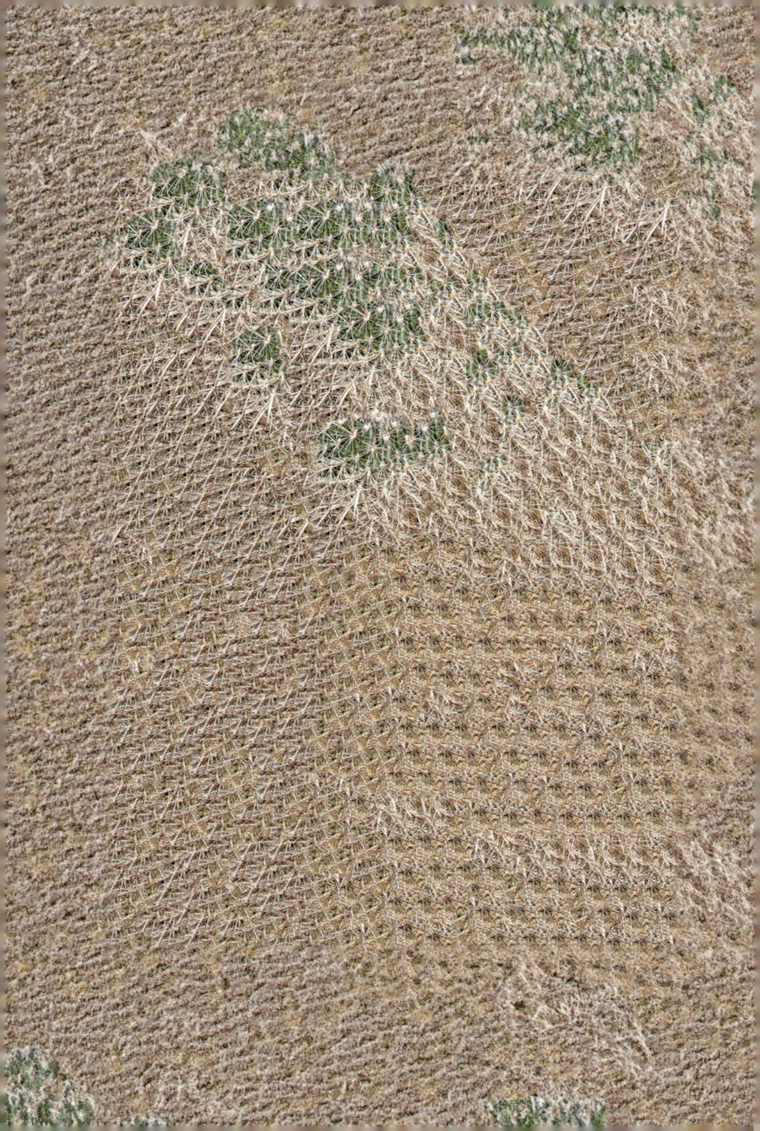

17.10.20

white psychosis
the anti racists
get called racists
a two volume set
of war and peace

11.10.20

mask on mask off
a wet paint sign
hanging round my neck
a love bite from
my childhood sweetheart

29.10.20

taking tea
in the shade of a lime tree
bees and flies
their zipper gets caught
for the umpteenth time

23.10.20

a bucketful of windfalls
served up with custard
the morning rush
Dad heads off early
to the power station

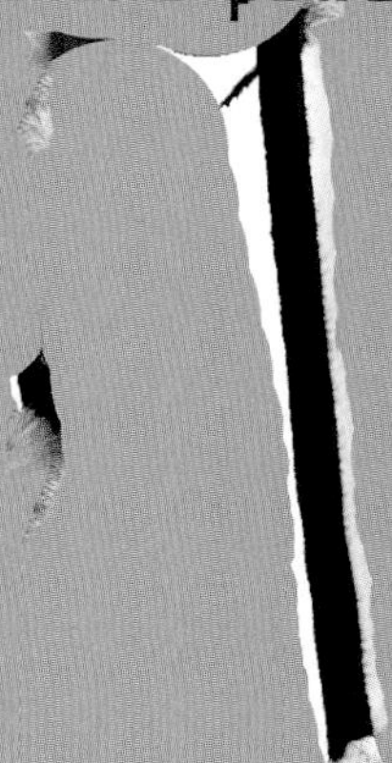

29.10.20

in his spare time
Marcus saves children
from cruel governments
the magician pulls
a packed lunch out of his hat

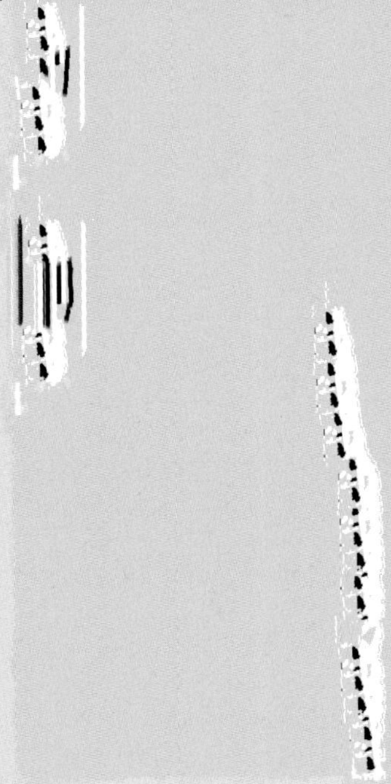

5.11.20

Autumn leaves turn
the public should be alert
but not alarmed
Somewhere in the distance
the smoke of something

31.10.20

am I next?
new rules mess me up
on a daily basis
he separates the red
from the yellow leaves

8.11.20

garden fireworks
honking and cheering
on Pennsylvanian streets
a golden shower
for Mr. President

8.11.20 Stella writes a poem
about the president's
mother's vagina
we white water raft
the Grand Canyon

6.11.20 if R above 1
his quick maths often
gets him out of trouble
a freezer full of buy one
get one free pizzas

8.11.20

four seasons
total landscaping
the depths of despair
a King Sago Palm
inherited from mum

8.11.20

climb every mountain
disrupt social norms
and criticise those in power
the sound of music
from a disused warehouse

13.11.20

people bragging
about the ending
of free movement
the meeting agrees
we need more fibre

12.11.20

all evening long
lipreading the spirits
red and yellow leaves
learning about whirling
dervishes on zoom

14.11.20

fallen leaves
the sound of the last post
filtered by oak trees
the email disclaimer
troubles him

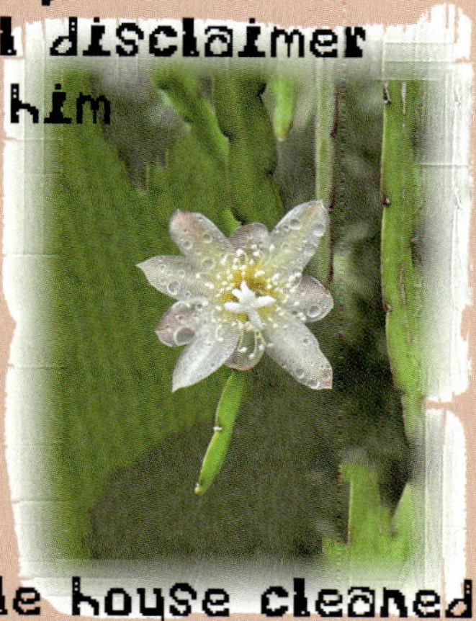

14.11.20

the whole house cleaned
a small victory
of light over darkness
a chalk dust pattern
on every doorstep

26.11.20

Tier 3 sucks
air particles squeeze
through gallery doors
the bouncer asks
to see my credentials

15.11.20

even hearts of oak fall
in the heat of battle
warm breath on cold air
our new kettle's light
turns from red to blue

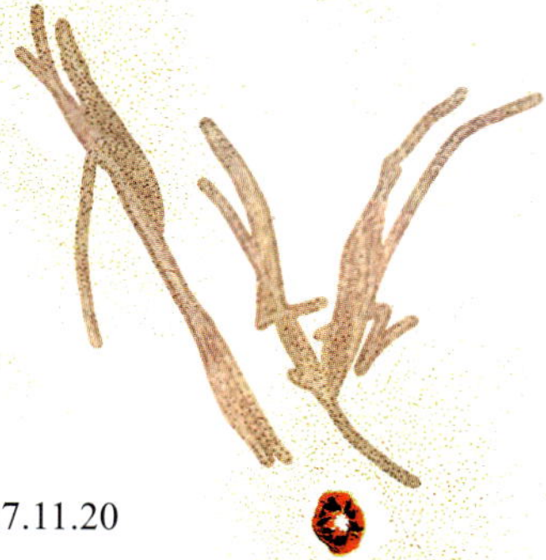

27.11.20

cold flirting
two woodpeckers jumping
up the tree of heaven
they buy a house in Camden
a glass and metal love nest

2.12.20

first sleet
crows and magpies
circle the playground
up close with Squarepusher
in the sweat of The Blue Note

30.11.20

wanted urgently
by a student
art and culture
the young couple carry
one child two loans

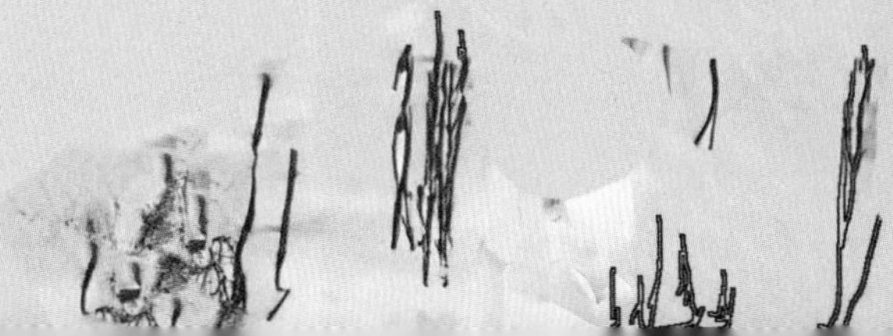

24.12.20

post Covid haze
a small gang of goldfinches
peck at next doors birch
a call goes up
one tree to another

6.12.20 (after Lady Skollie)

camouflaging cars
they don't hijack u for it
they shoot u dead
a photo of his firstborn
tucked in his wallet

30.12.20

red sky at morning
we unfreeze the locks
and put the kettle on
her beautiful mess of curls
all over my face

25.1.21

in the world
of inanimate objects
a nest
deep in the sandstone
the bee catcher carves

7.1.21

fresh cat shit
the return of my senses
after covid 19
Sada Kichi
the two of us forever

6.1.21

old wrongs new
sounds more enn you I
than on we
the heavy bedding
undulates and lifts

31.1.21

before the pub
Dad beats up the Yorkshire puds
his bricklayer hands
beneath the floorboards
a cat's skeleton

27.1.21

problematic books
the poet Kerimi dies
in Chinese prison
never underestimate
the power of words

12.2.21

the vicar's collar
a house big enough
for ten rough sleepers
our cat licks out
the empty tuna tin

3.2.21

on the blood machine
getting chatted up
by all the nurses
a cup of sweet tea
and a digestive biscuit

21.2.21

from daffodils
to deprivation
master of reality
yellow bellied birds
crowd the branches

21.2.21

so alive alive
cockles and muscles
for dinner and tea
bivalved beings divide
agitate and conquer

21.2.21

win win lose
low low high
nothing live die
treble twenty
followed by the bull

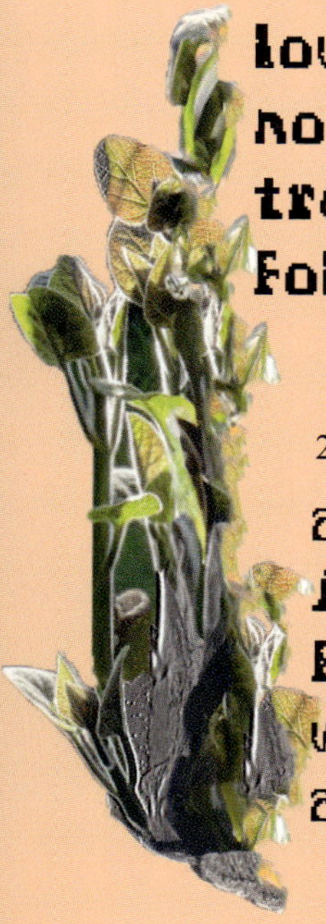

21.2.21

an old soul
in a young head
fish heads and tails
wiping himself down
after getting steamed

4.3.21

the disease is hosted
by an organised community
each morning at six
Brother John wakes the boys
with sacred murmurings

2.3.21

you sailed you failed
adapting the machinery
of global travel
we grab on for dear life
to the edge of the Earth

24.2.21

an empty nest
found in the winter wood
my father's boots
trying to organise
the mess in my head

10.3.21

the wind and the rain
slithers of sunlight passing
through blackthorn blossom
shedding my skin
with a little wiggle

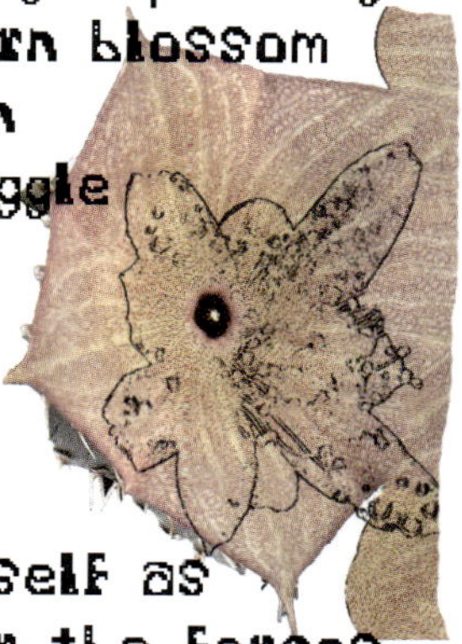

10.3.21

visualise yourself as
an antennae for the forces
of the multiverse
twitching with the ants
high up in the branches

21.3.21

blossom viewing
just one more slice
of lemon drizzle cake
a twenty sided dice
in my pocket

11.3.21

first blossom
a small poem passing
hut to hut
roam if you want to
roam around the world

8.4.21

their first kiss
the taste of cherry blossom
on her bottom lip
a bighorn ram
nuts a barrel cactus

27.3.21

River Avon chills
policing defaults
to random assault
the sound of batons
on riot shields and heads

21.3.21

kill the bill
the police just need
to just back off
we try to define
a public nuisance

18.4.21

days weeks years
her mind a lost child
honeysuckle
an embrace of vibrations
guides the bee on

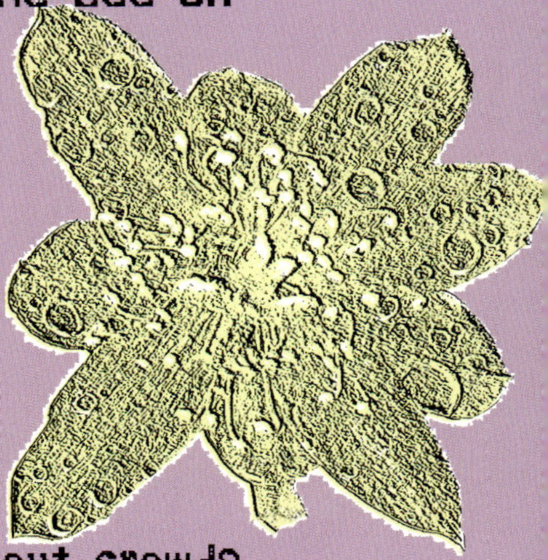

15.4.21

a year without crowds
novel booze consumption
outside in the cold
she says it's the fire in
her belly keeps her going

3.5.21

everyday problems
araucaria
araucana
we see no hear no
and speak no evil

23.4.21

a bag of sugar
and a rhubarb stick
a boy again
floating minerals welcomed
by Earth's gravity

4.5.21

street furniture
don't crush my spirit
with pains and torment
our brother breaks his arm
when we're not looking

4.5.21

talking loudly
a pheasant flies up
from the heather
patterned masks cut
from an African fabric

14.5.21

our parting kiss
a mixture of salt
and sweet peppers
an ultimatum
from the university

10.5.21

a third poet
tortured and killed
in Myanmar
a plumber a joiner
a librarian

8.5.21

mayflowers
all night dancing
to a dead beat
firecracker spicy ribs
and egg fried rice

21.5.21

free Palestine
no more slow prison
of sustainable calm
a hill covered with rockrose
soft and wild and sweet smelling

21.5.21

we lose ourselves
in deep meditation
a crack in the rocks
stepping out of the page
into the sensual world

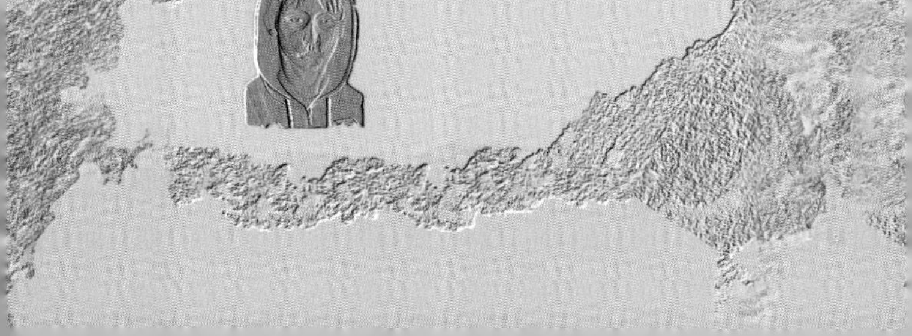

27.5.21

you and I are earth
forged by the sun
water from the sky
purple faced pansies
self seeded and strong

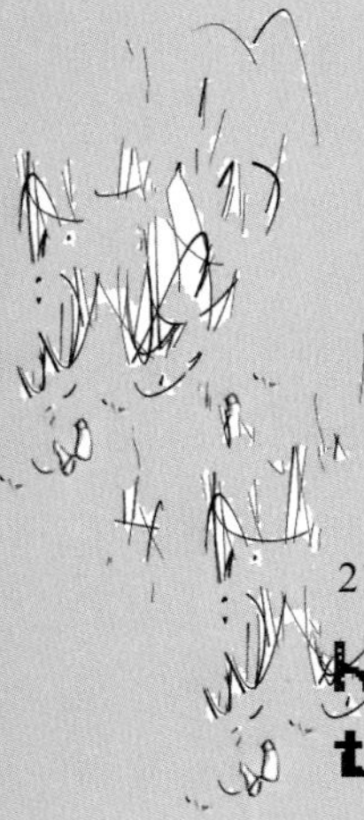

26.5.21

wild swimming
a rush of adrenaline
cuts through the lake
the dramaturgy
of this landscape

21.5.21

hot morning bath
the horrors
of Israel's suprematism
how the water flows
stream river sea

29.5.21

we pull over
for a toilet stop and lunch
desert rose
erecting the tent
looking stripping kissing

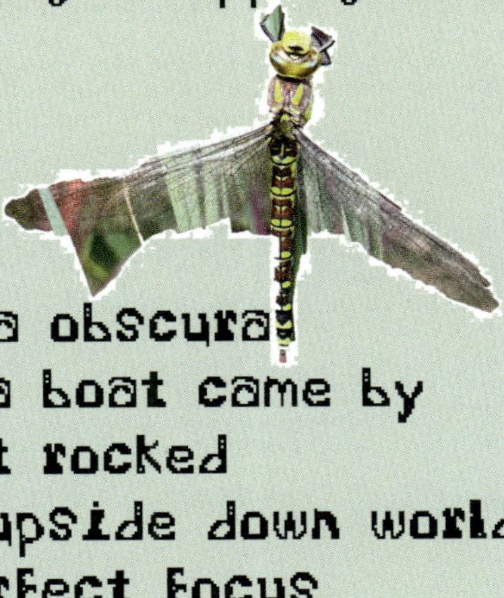

28.5.21

camera obscura
then a boat came by
and it rocked
this upside down world
in perfect focus

16.6.21

Sometimes
we just have to let it go
grass cuttings
the heat of the compost
attracts the worms

2.6.21

icebergs and bird song
a conversation
with you about us
even unsinkable ships
Sometimes go down

29.5.21

Stag's antlers
covered in soft velvet
unfurling fern
the Bishop condemns
Israel's long apartheid

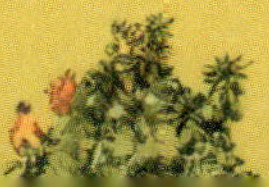

7.7.21

snow country
the difference between
a good girl and a good woman
removing all borders
from our minds

6.7.21

new variant factories
a hug a kiss
a touch of your hand
we sing together
at grandad's wake

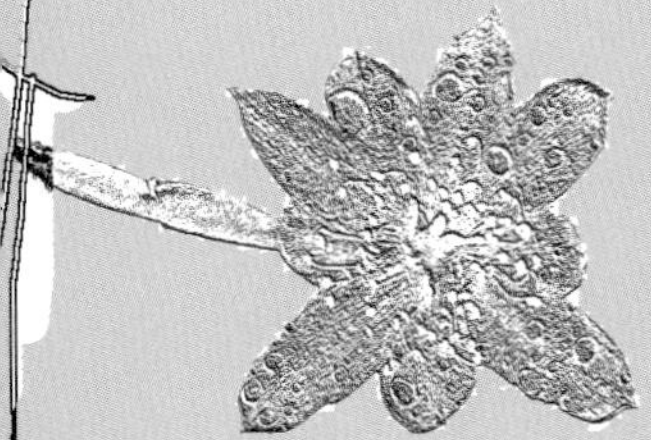

9.7.21

crowning
I want to pop my head
out of your orifice
the landlady serves notice
on our tenancy

8.7.21

penalties
the long walk
to the slaughterhouse
Delroy Wilson's
Riding for a Fall

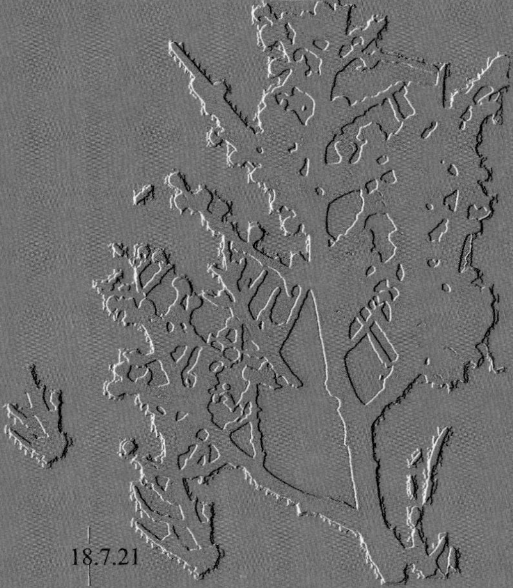

18.7.21

a photograph
of the universe
burned onto my body
negative to positive
in thirty minutes flat

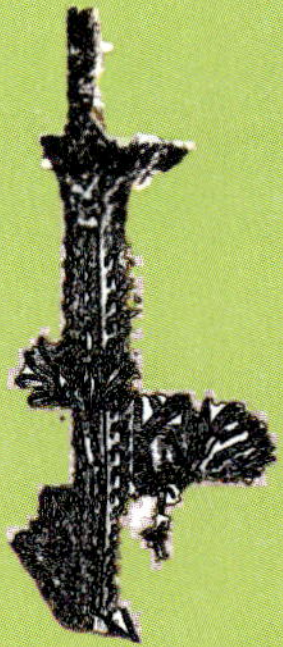

26.7.21

don't hate the drip
a jar of explosives
to feed the plants
tendrils of hop
probe the kitchen window

21.7.21

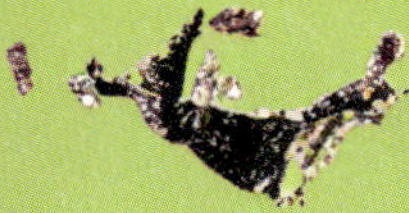

after the mowing
a Cherry Bakewell
and a cup of sweet tea
buzzing up the anthers
stigma and style

10.8.21

folding her love
into a paper animal
the end of summer
a dirty plaster
hanging from his thumb

4.8.21

over Frankly Beeches
five heavy slabs
in the back of the car
what's under the patio
stays under the patio

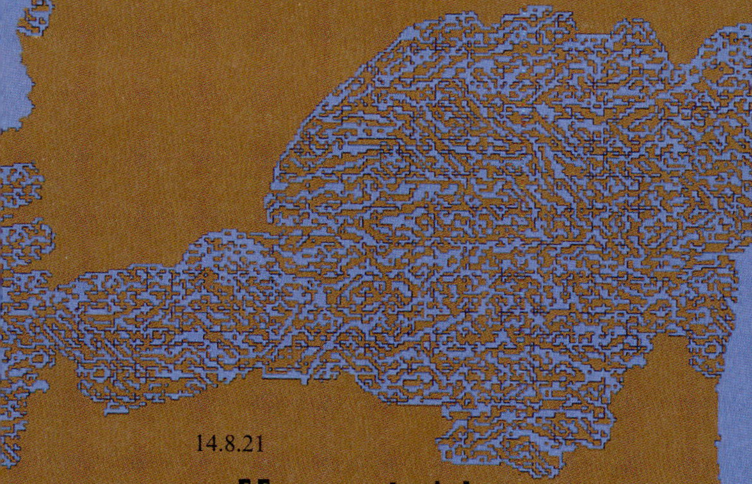

14.8.21

coffee outside
a passerby we don't know
gives us a wave
the website calculates
our carbon footprint

13.8.21

made for each other
anniversary cards
with owls bees jigsaws and tits
some plants just seem
to grow well together

22.8.21

you got a lot
bromeliads coming
out of your armpits
a poison arrow frog
in the palm of my hand

14.8.21

day dream believer
lily pollen
on a white shirt
poetry is removed
from the curriculum

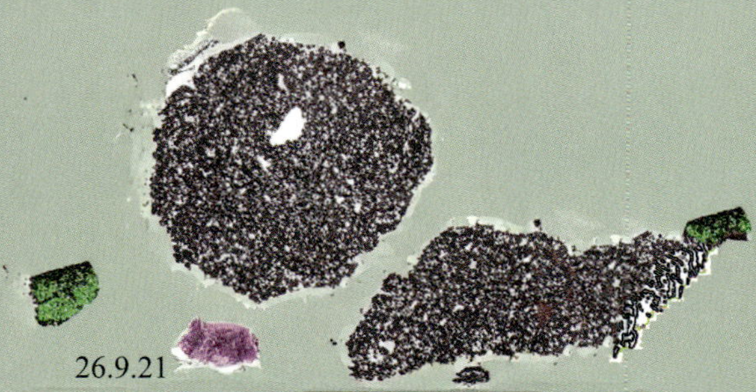

26.9.21

the plant hunter
swiping adenium
to zanthoxylum
John the Younger
brings home a tulip tree

18.9.21

Yoko smashes it
Bas Jan drops it
mending the past
an ancient tea bowl
of gold filled cracks

13.10.21

halfway up the hill
a jay stealing an acorn
from a grey squirrel
every time I shave
I get younger

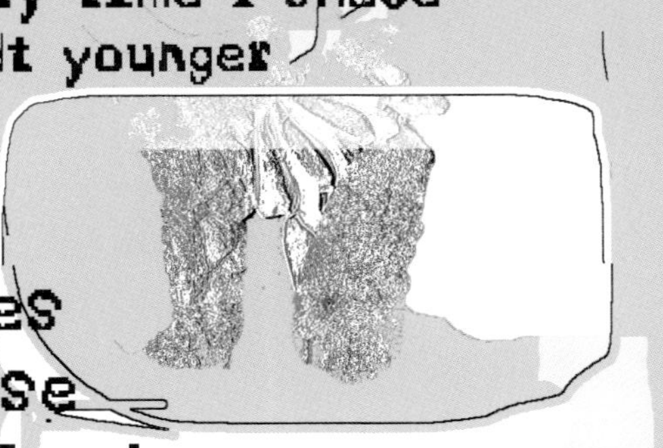

12.10.21

olives
cheese
cat food
the mice fail
at their first attempt

16.11.21

autumn grasses
if my love won't come to me
I'll go to them
his best friend's betrayal
comes into focus

31.10.21

the dentist's chair
between the drilling
a blackbird
checking routines
and micro aggressions

29.11.21

thunderheads
the stench of zen
and damp soil
lighting up the glasshouse
with some old paraffin

25.11.21

dad shows off
his ornamental banana
the night sky blushes
polishing the silverware
with an old cloth

24.11.21

preparing for winter
a trail of banana leaves
in her wake
the old poet moves hut
just one more time

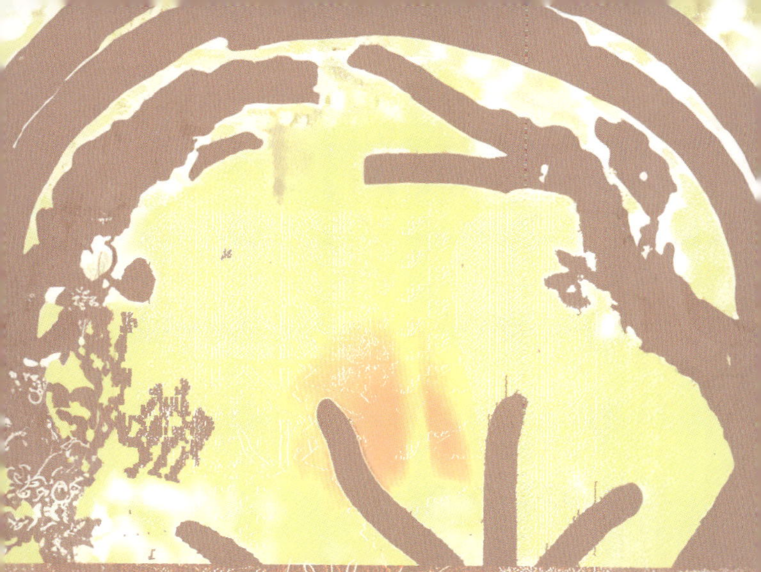

29.11.21

sealing up
the cold lips of a troll
this winter wind
a nail in the post
for next years squash

4.12.21

bread and roses
a young woman
talks loudly into her watch
the harvest is always richer
in other fields

3.12.21

elixir of life
Maciek swaps the tuna
for an eel nigiri
we wriggle and rock
on our bar stools

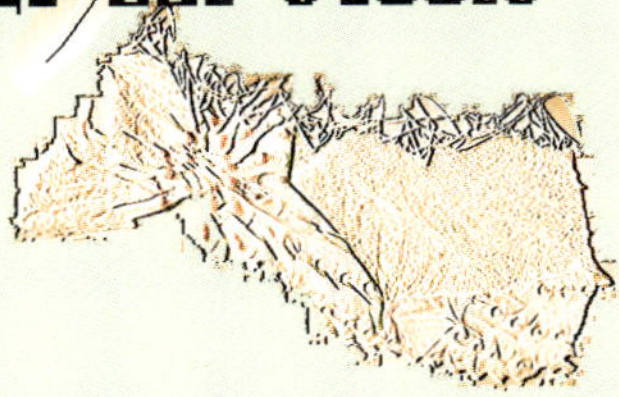

14.12.21

do not think
that you didn't count
winter warmers
two pints of infinity
and a pork pie

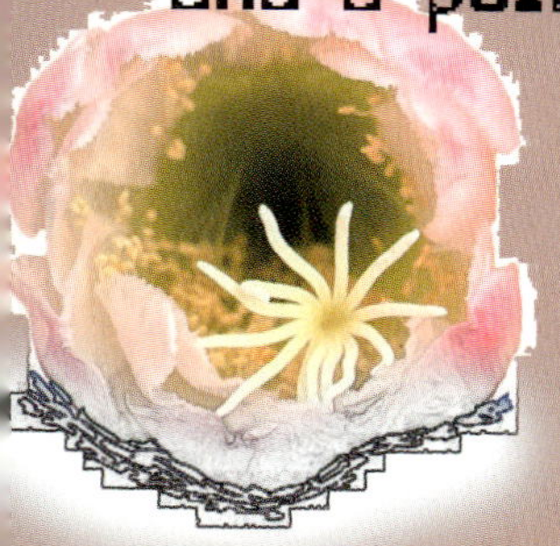

4.12.21

after the boiling room
breathing in the heat
and sweet scent of crabs
next time she says
I'll wear a sweatband

27.5.23

Soft rain
I try to describe
what I can't see
Laura only follows
eighteen people

20.12.21

pub grub and drinks
a man shows me
a photograph of his dog
burrowing into
the hard drive's core

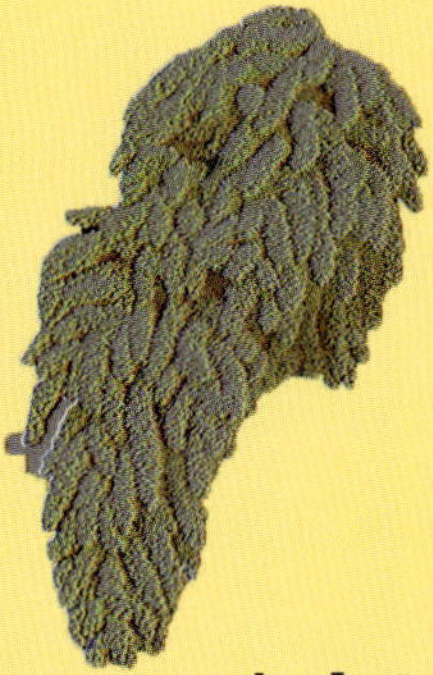

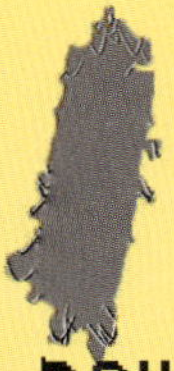

23.12.21

longest night
every day from now
a little bit brighter
playing AFX at
33 then 45

21.12.21

viral knitwear
a zoom meeting
of Christmas jumpers
pay attention to yours
and others' mental health

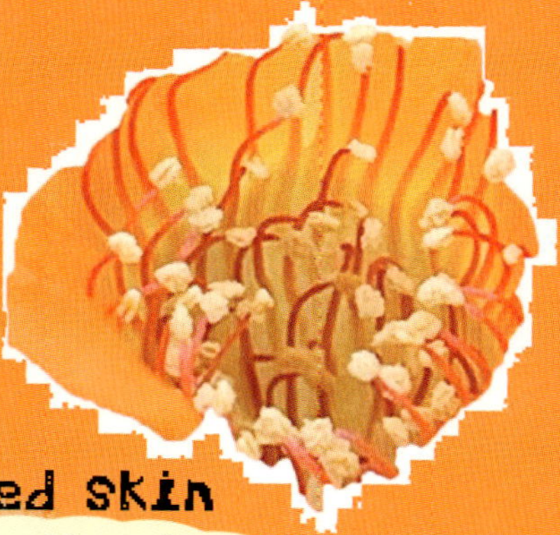

3.1.22

smoked skin
after the New Year's
garden party
twixt heaven and hell
we spit into the abyss

26.12.21 (after Bashō)

I envy clouds
the heavy burden
of worldly belongings
a double rainbow
over the old steelworks

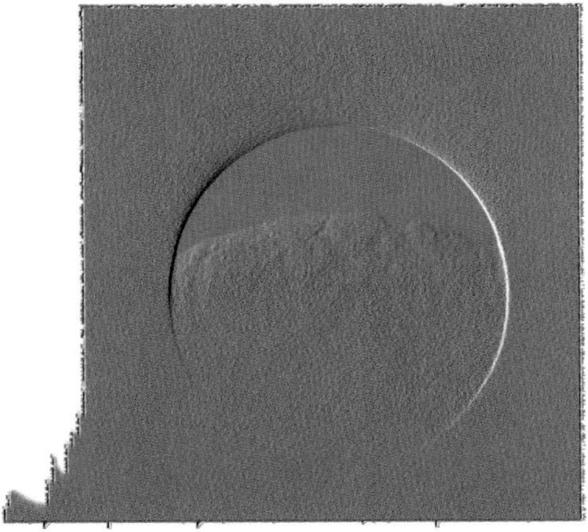

6.1.22 we ride out the night
into the dawn chorus
eagles and sparrows
all booms and lights
on Saint Sebastian

3.1.22 (after Etel Adnan)

this is the way
the universe works
a seed a pea a lentil
a hand reaching up
from the primordial soup

15.1.22

every work of art
a request for love
and attention
thoughts become words
in the day long fog

7.1.22

is it possible
to make admin free art
asking for a friend
coke or coke zero?
it's all a matter of taste

21.1.22

driving rain
the sax on the bridge
plays into the night
the curve of her back
glistening heat

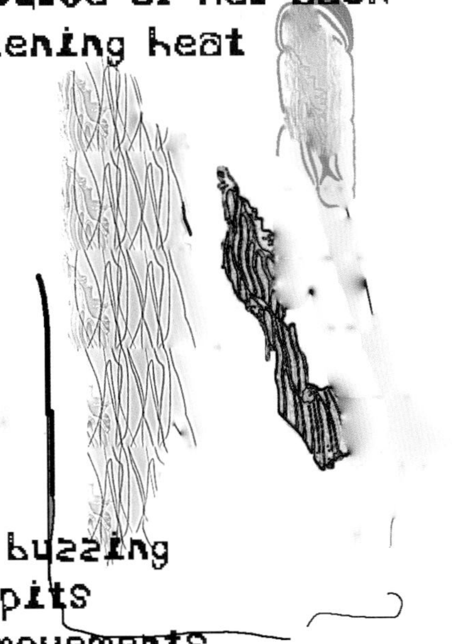

20.1.22

freshen up
tie fighters buzzing
round my armpits
we plan our movements
Wookey Hole then Cheddar Gorge

26.1.22

you burn me
let the water run
for a very long time
she sheds one skin
to reveal another

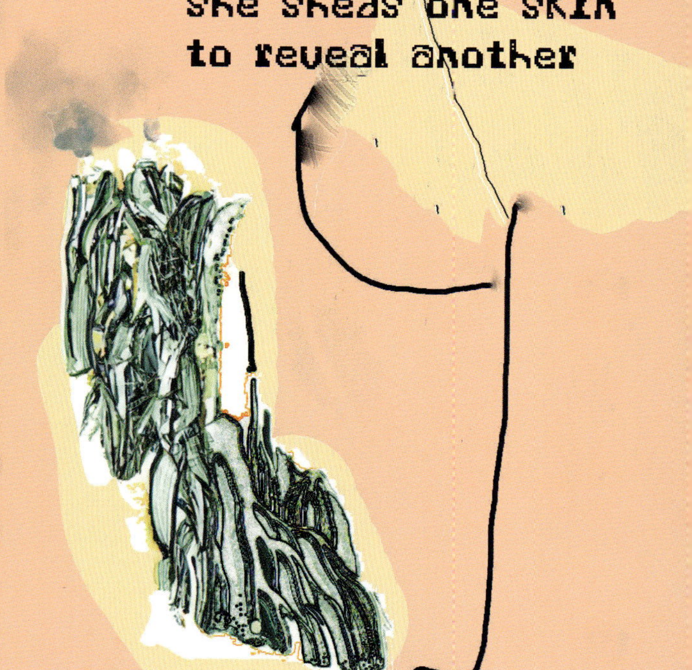

1.2.22

swinging Loughborough
paparazzi
in the singer's kitchen
a pile of car keys
on the coffee table

27.1.22

racists post stickers
on our code of conduct
fear and psychosis
together we make
doorstep rangoli

11.2.22

the sphincter relaxes
around the lumen
teetering governments
a pair of red stilettos
from the dressing up box

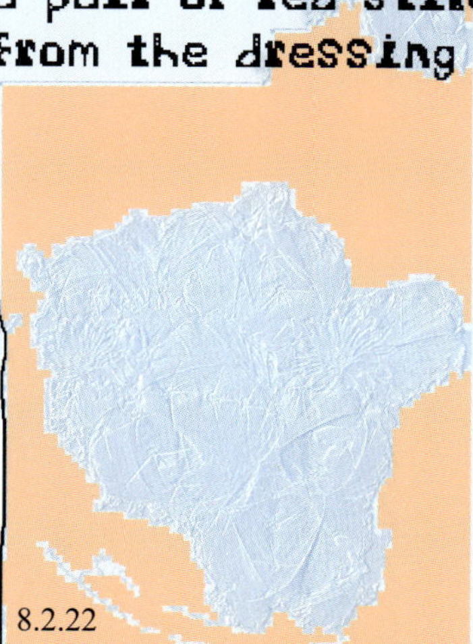

8.2.22

a slight rearrangement
of the gallery walls
suddenly milder
a young man in a hoody
hands me my wallet

19.2.22 (after Dan Graham)

rolling video
performer audience
mirror
sometimes it's hard
to tell left from right

18.2.22

waiting for the storm
an early morning meet up
with the market chairs
we baton down the hatches
with a vegan full english

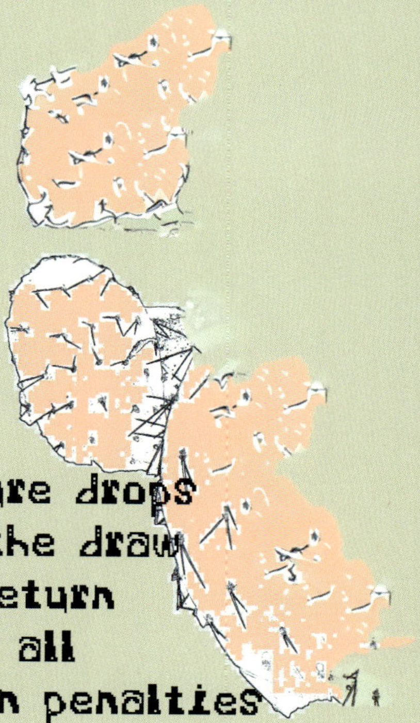

13.3.22

my pressure drops
between the draw
and the return
to cap it all
we lose on penalties

24.2.22

a cold wind blowing
there are few die well
that die in a battle
a little sparkle
down in the darkness

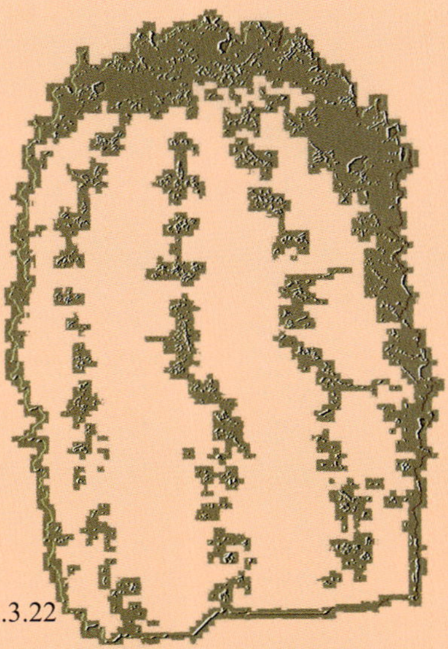

13.3.22

last night's kebab
and a bowl of cornflakes
wind blown daffodils
slicing through the husks
of the old palm tree

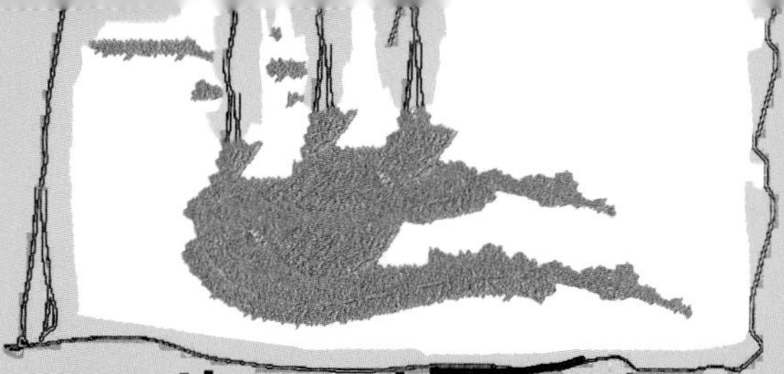

19.3.22

three drinks in
we talk about words
clitoris
my dancing comes
as a big surprise

19.3.22

pitching up tents
in the back garden
summer sleepover
a pile of jazz magazines
under grandad's bed

13.3.22

I steal a kiss
from Agatha Christie
the mystery of flowers
a virus clinging
to my fingertips

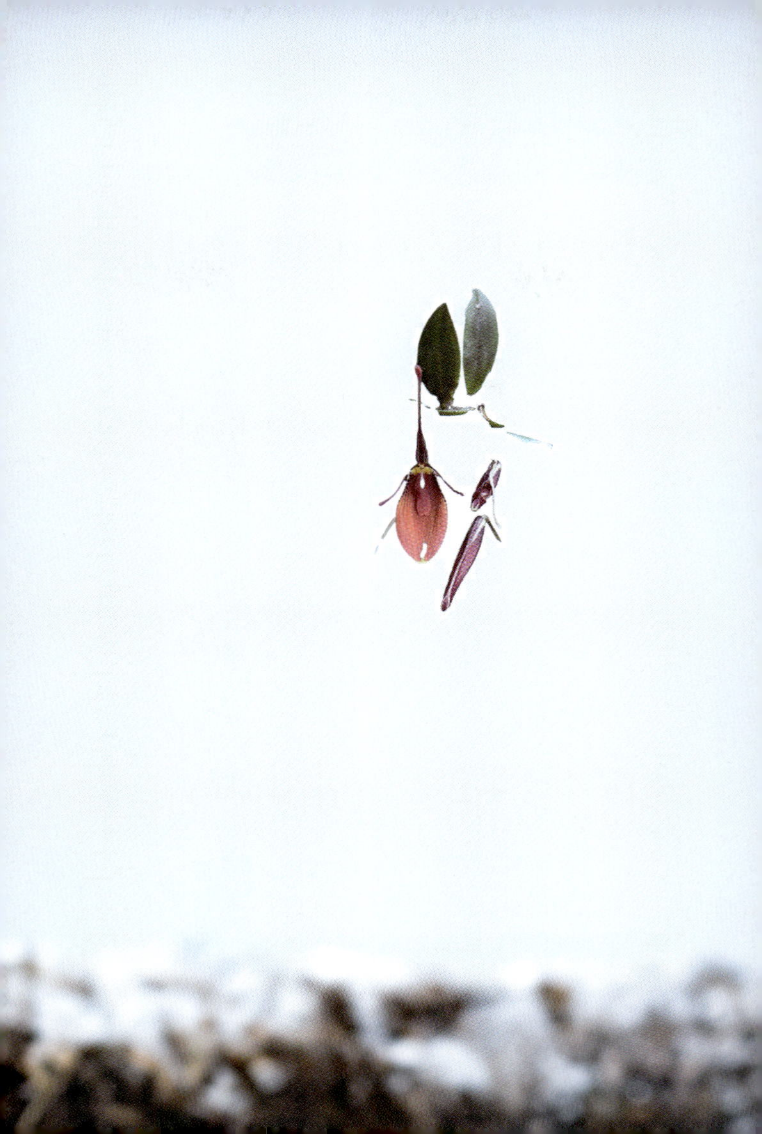

21.3.22

turning from she fox
to princess and back again
the season changes
stripping the old husks
from our trachycarpus

21.3.22

a history of progress
transforming empire
into empathy
all these years thinking
I know what you're feeling

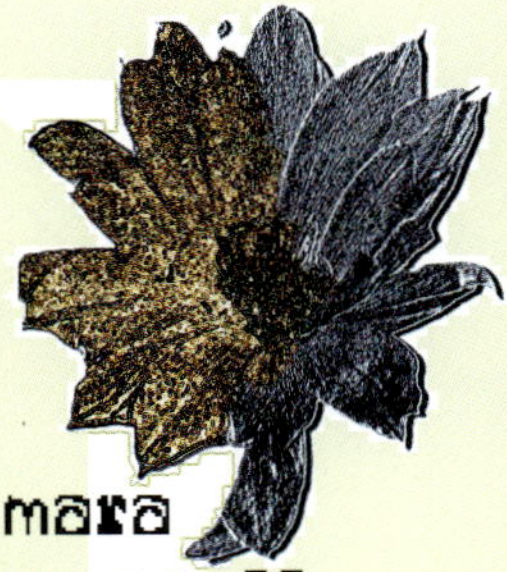

2.4.22

second hand max mara
I've got some radge stuff
on my ebay watch
Pam and Tommy stop a while
to clean the camera lens

21.3.22

feels like spring
a policewoman asks me
if I'm alright
on the rebound
I find my true love

4.4.22

time and tide
wait for no man
we plant onions
a worm's eye view
beneath the permaculture

13.4.22

the same people
flying out to Venice
like it's all the same
his type is offset
and certificated

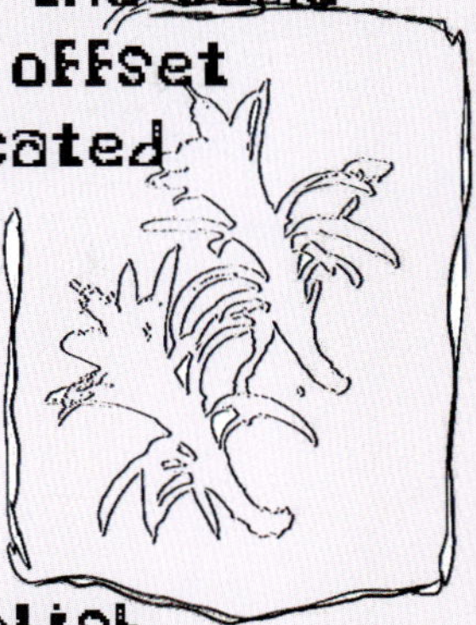

6.4.22

rubbing shoe polish
into warm tired leather
dad's old golf clubs
stare back at me
from the back of the garage

14.4.22

until nothing's left
another stone caught
in the tread of my shoe
a snake's head fritillary
harbouring a bumblebee

13.4.22

no apology
you did it
and you've got to go
the whole hill taken
by rhododendrons

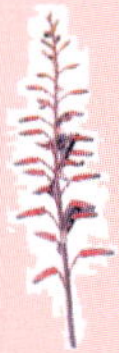

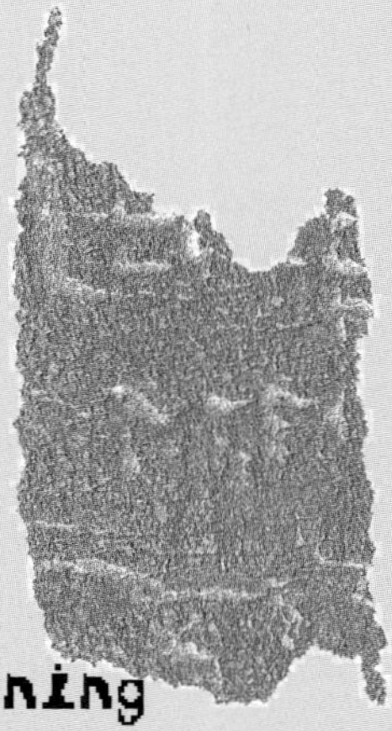

20.4.22

new morning
the katydid in my head
tells me a story
secret shapes revealed
by the first mow of the year

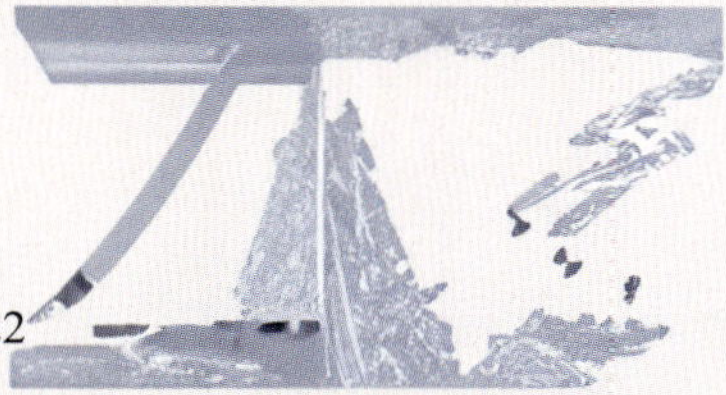

26.4.22

stroking my stubble
razorbill eggs
on the Isle of May
the sphynx cat scratches
both my inner thighs

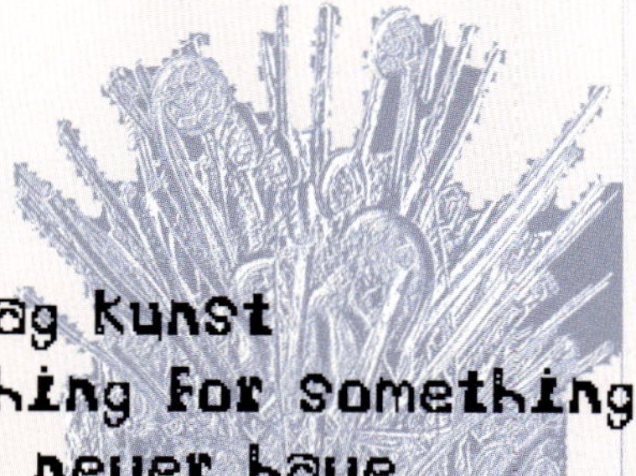

24.4.22

hashtag kunst
searching for something
I will never have
this year we decide to
let the dandelions be

5.5.22

looking up
ammonium nitrate
for my poetry
a fourth of dad's plot
is purple and white clover

29.4.22

without your love
will I ever write
a better line
the landlord smears vaseline
on the bog's flat surfaces

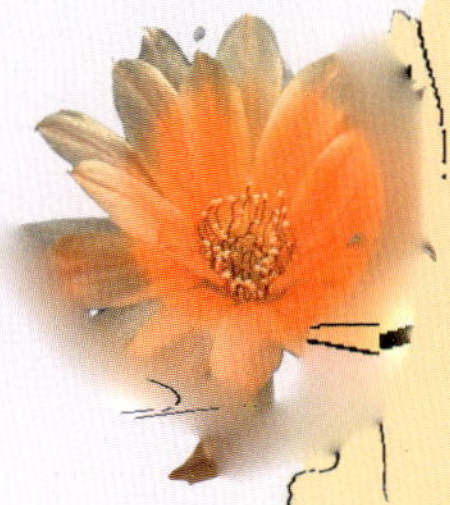

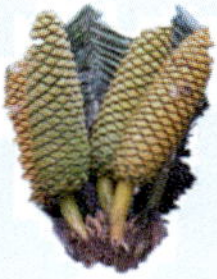

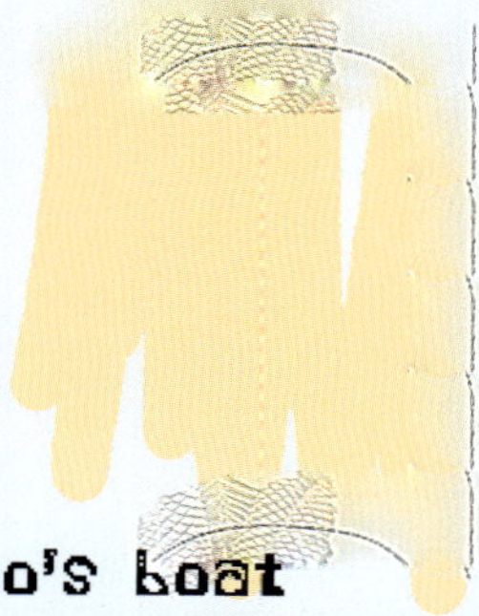

16.6.22

Dom and Bruno's boat
filled with sacks of earth
sinking into the river
caddisfly larvae ensconced
in sticks and stones

6.6.22

no confidence
the clown's makeup
leaves nasty stains
the face on the egg
stares blankly back

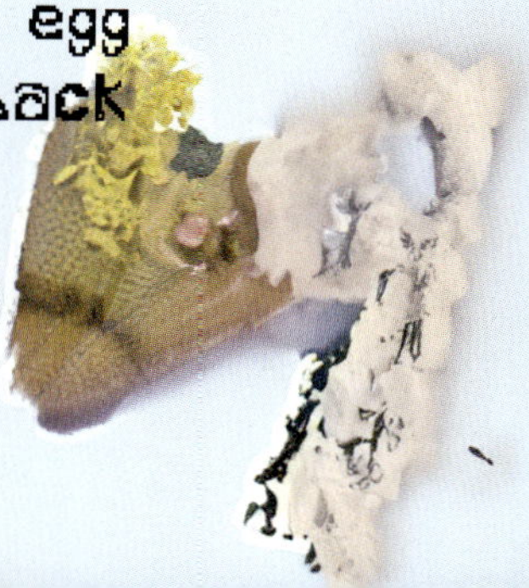

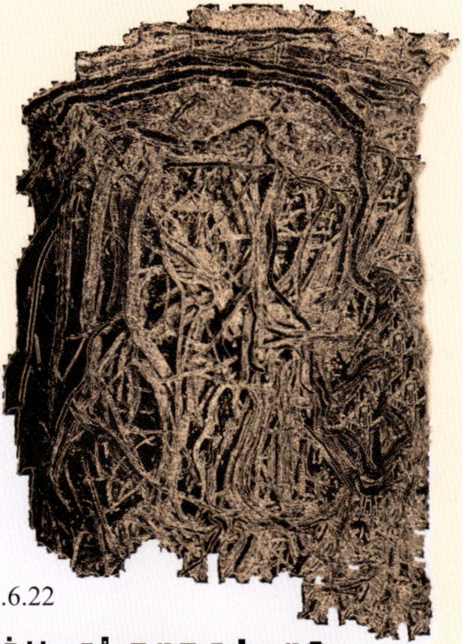

21.6.22

six characters
in search of a plant
that tends for itself
her roots are in the air
not the soil

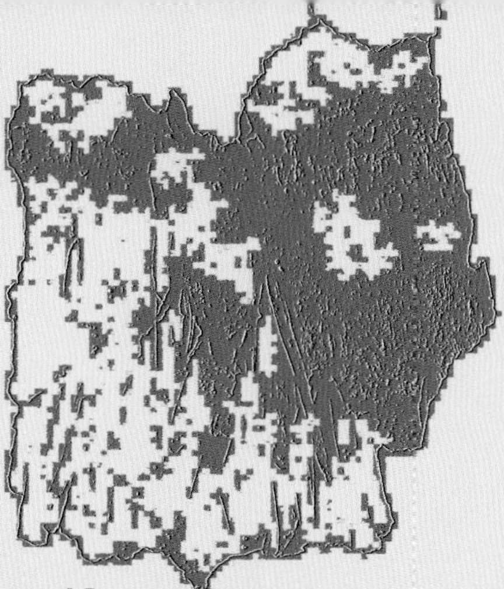

25.6.22

love rail workers
protect the human
right to say no
you can tell your little friend
it's time to go

24.6.22

a feather
in amongst the clover
anthracite
working together
for victory

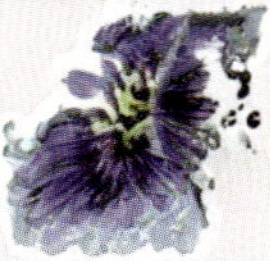

25.6.22

an uppercut
that I never saw coming
foxglove
you ease my heart
and soothe my eyes

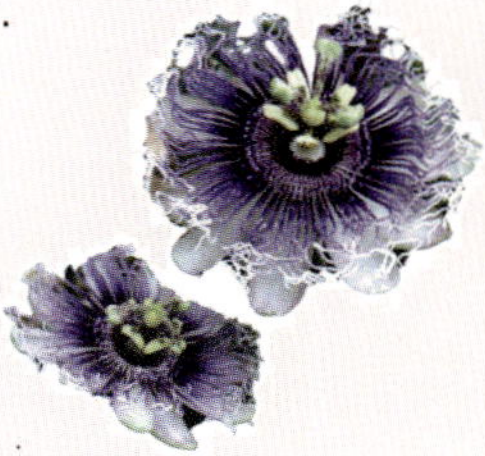

13.7.22

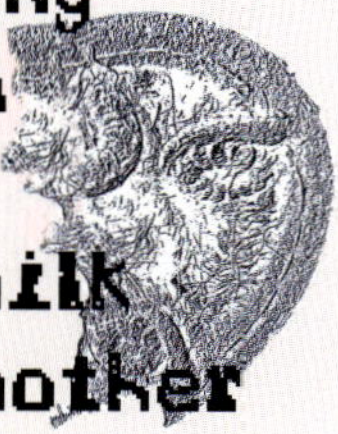

slowly unpacking
Barbie and Ken
the east wind
drinking the milk
of a Pashtun mother

7.7.22

them's the breaks
the unravelling
of rotting privilege
from two step to grime
the dance floor erupts

29.6.22

she tells me the horse
won't come when you shout it
a wolf whistle
around men they always
feel uncomfortable

13.7.22

long shadows
the guys at the car wash
talk about home
another cover up
by the Foreign Office

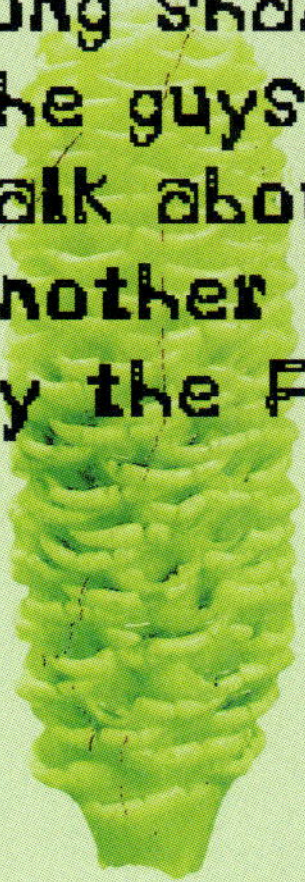

17.7.22 the morning sun
reddens my arms
an adder's back
this week I'm struggling
to make ends meet

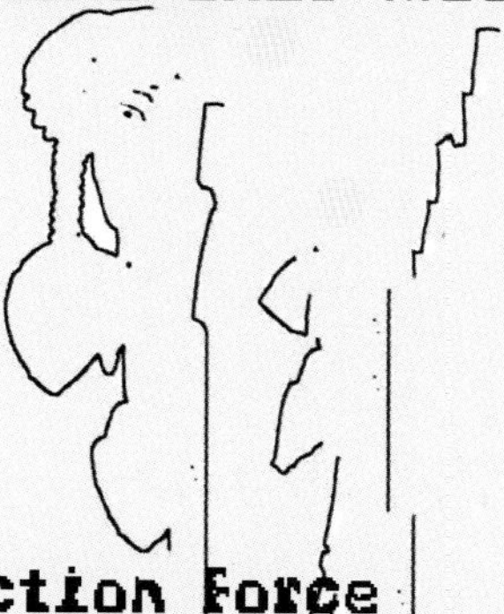

15.7.22

protection force
a new phase of corporate
colonial ultraviolence
patting its own back
the universal self

21.7.22 on the slate
the focus puller
wins all the awards
a crow and a magpie
in deep conversation

20.7.22

T junction
I turn and follow
the morning sun
it cuts deeper
than anyone can know

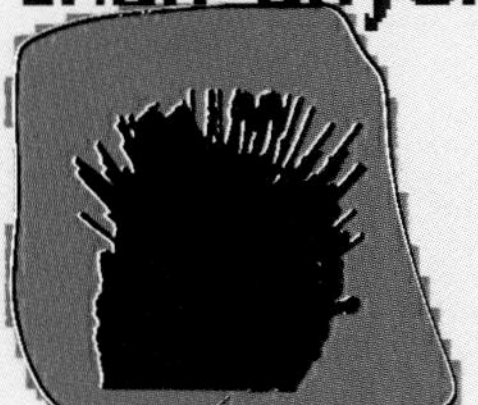

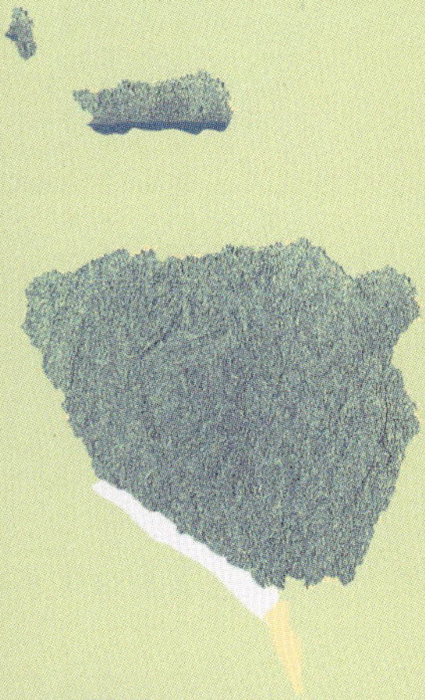

23.7.22

guns at the station
my city gears up
for some empire games
we unroll an old world map
of countries coloured in red

3.8.22 we lament being broke
why do your bars rhyme
when mine don't
slowly we march back
to the top of the hill

2.8.22

we eat our lunch
under an old willow
whispering wasps
live fire exercises
over the Taiwan Strait

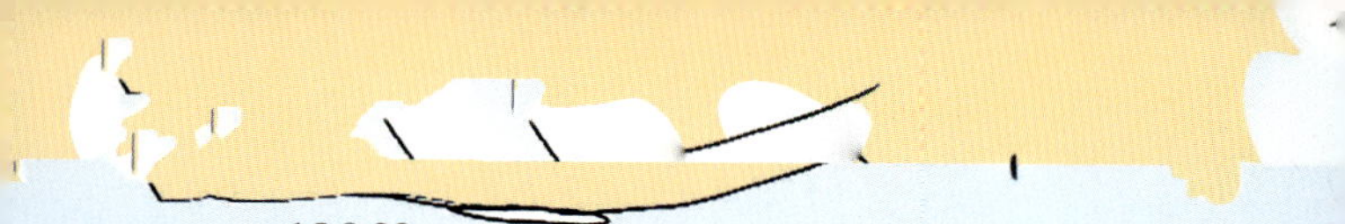

15.8.22

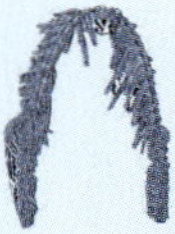

the counter revolution
appears from nowhere
a cuckoo chick
thrown out of the nest
by hedge sparrows

15.8.22 (after Issa)

a green insect
and a brown insect
singing a duet
the counter revolution
appears from nowhere

25.8.22

I plant everyday
five or six ideas
in search of you
summer grasses
rustling in the breeze

22.8.22

I don't know quite what
I'd do without my glasses
early falling leaves
Pilkington's takes control
of Chance Brothers and Co

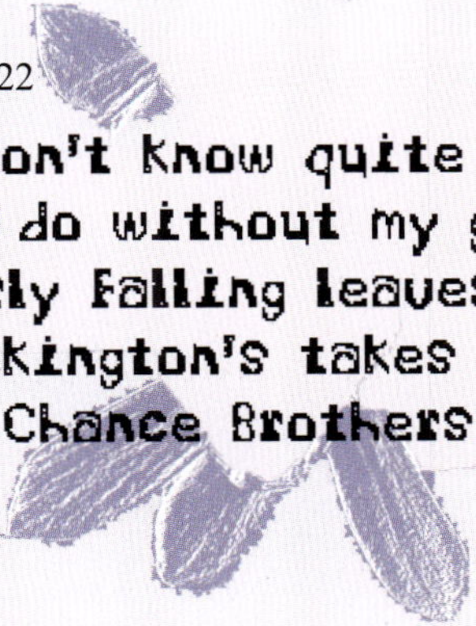

10.9.22

she reaches in
and pulls something out
interior scroll
a rabbit a dove
the knave of hearts

10.9.22

falling leaves
what a lie looks like
on your lover's lips
widespread flooding
and forest fires

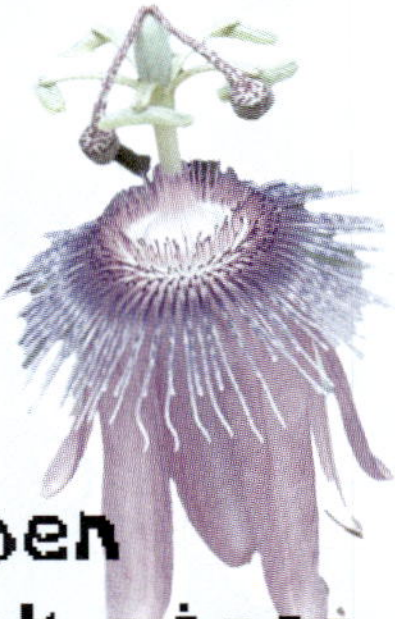

13.9.22

a marker pen
and a blank piece of paper
not my king
shiny shiny
boots of leather

12.9.22

tightening muscles
and dreaded breath
autumn arrives
a spider
with an angel on its back

19.9.22

autumn chill
the busker stops
to tune his guitar
plucking out needles
from my ponderosa pine

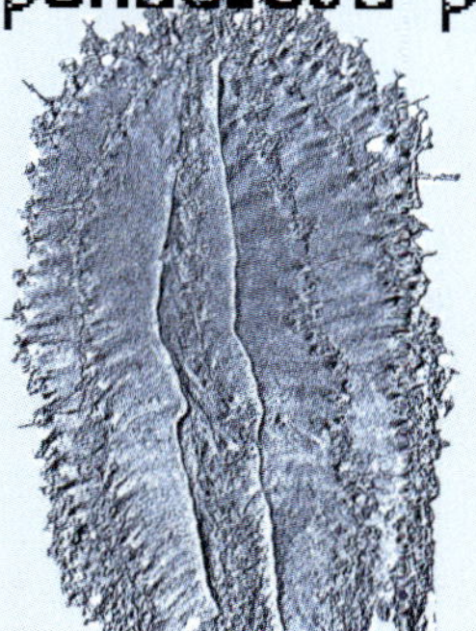

25.9.22

a Russian joke
told in Ukraine
into the lamplight
the jagged flight of a bat
up and down the close

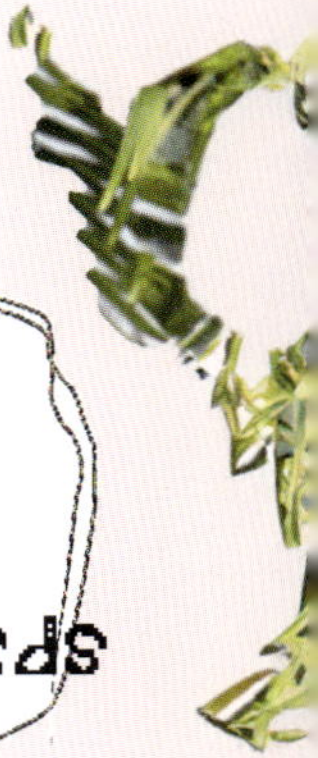

25.9.22

sea fret
I lose my bearings
on the beach
three and a half chords
played fast and hard

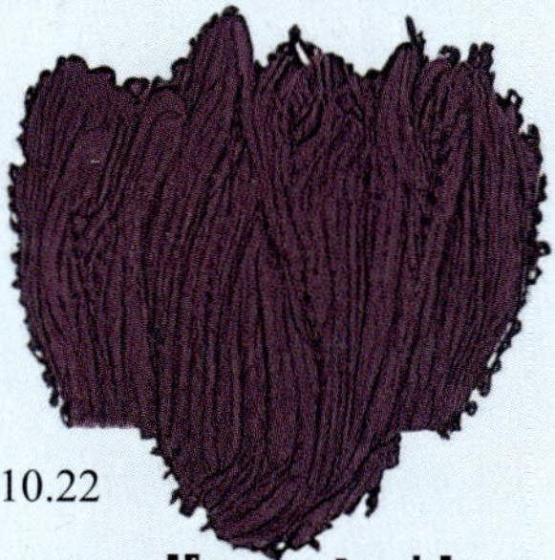

10.10.22

Conrad's strike
withdrawing labour
from this floating world
Wordsworth and dioxin
in a mountain stream

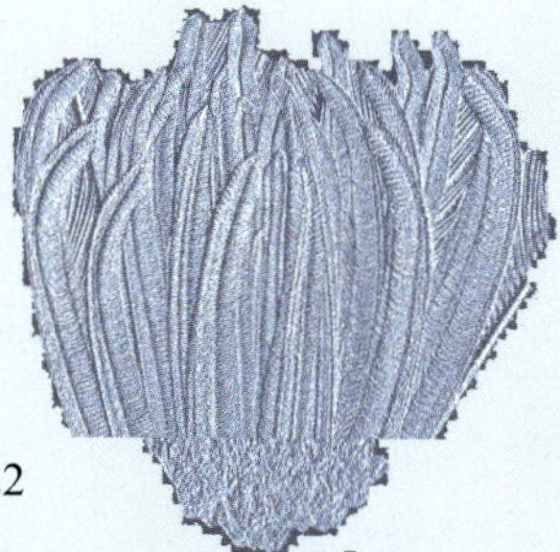

29.9.22

for my mother
for my daughter
scissors cutting hair
a bobcat chasing
a jackrabbit

18.10.22

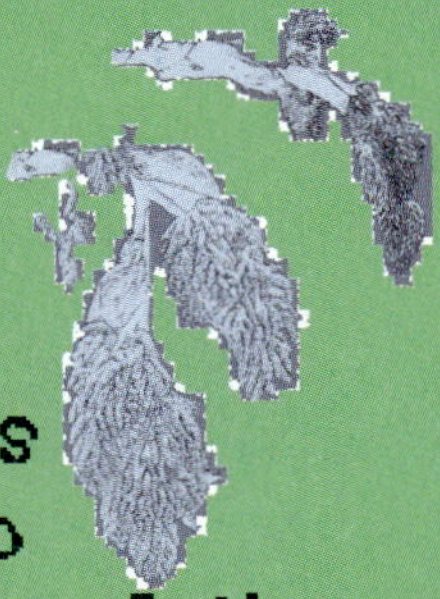

giant lobelias
on the way up
the mountains of the moon
the never ever ending
malaria death ledger

23.10.22

rolling out the plinth
dragging it back in
the pound goes up
some tuppenny rice
and half a pound of treacle

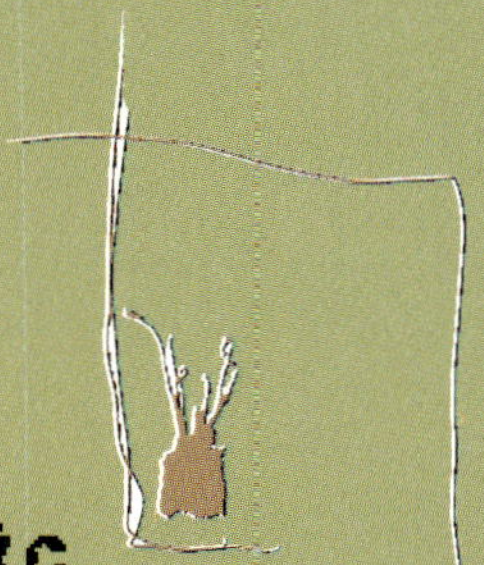

23.10.22

fly agaric
we walk on towards
the power station
a long list of treats
ready for the tuck shop

26.11.22

DJing
to an empty room
on top of the pub
up comes Uncle Ronnie
three sheets to the wind

6.11.22

one kind of luck
or another
crows in a tree
four trunks growing
out of an elephant's foot

31.10.22

last flap of the wings
a dragonfly skeleton
clinging to bubblewrap
dad eschews the pumpkin
and carves out a turnip

22.12.22

winter traveling
I accidentally leave
my coat in the car
the wolves nibble
at each other's necks

8.12.22

it don't make no sense
why you gonna dig up coal
when the sky's on fire
pink marshmallows
on a toasting fork

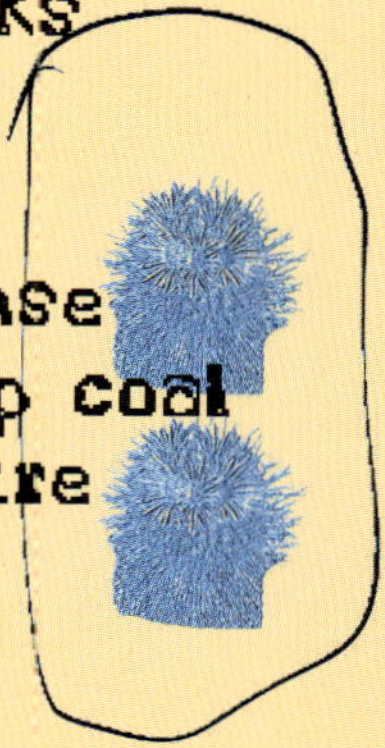

4.12.22

three imaginary boys
six different ways
a thousand hours
we fear for Tinkerbell
and her fading light

25.12.22

all through Christmas
we hold back guilty thoughts
soup kitchen steam
perfect pigs in blankets
and a pot of rice n peas

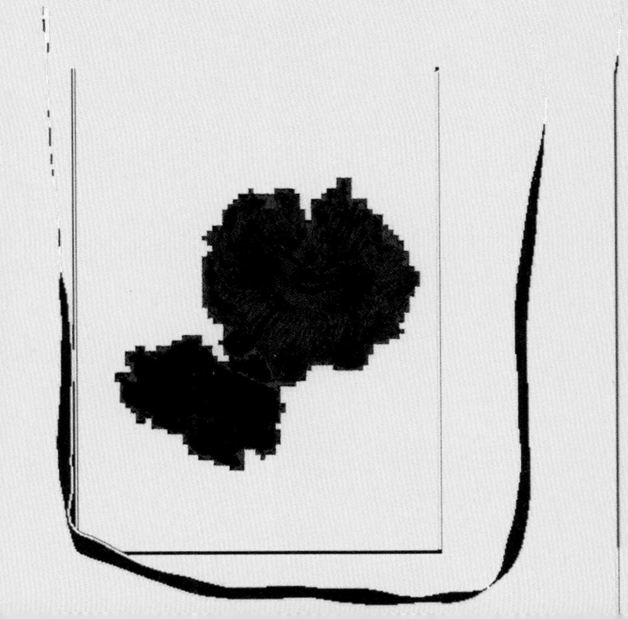

1.1.23

communing
living and dead
and soon to be
wilted roses
in a white vase

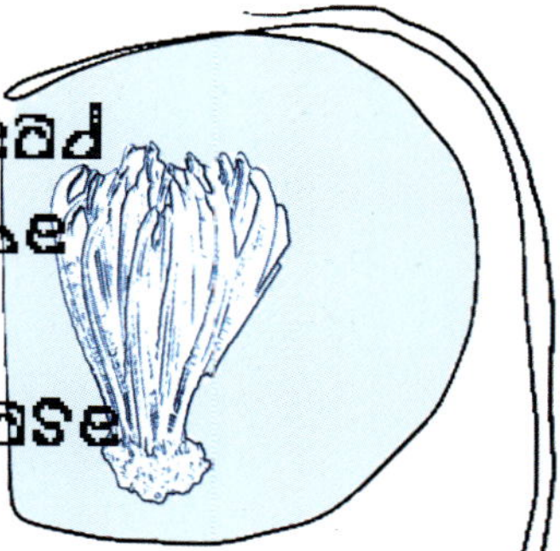

1.1.23

living is a thing
no one is safe
until everyone
sunflower hearts gather
below the bird table

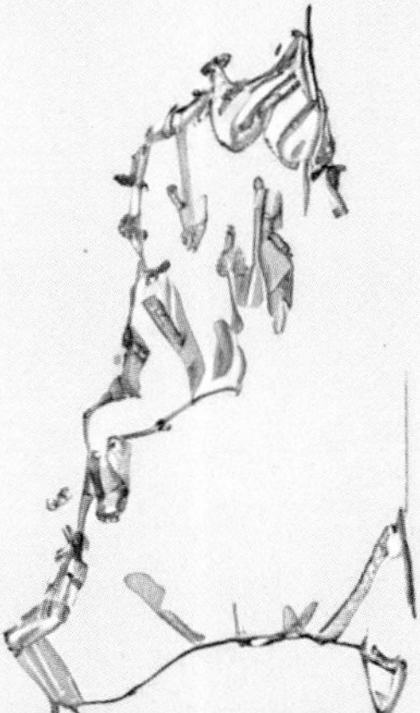

18.1.23

more class warfare
the government chooses
bankers over nurses
a sticking plaster floating
around the deep end

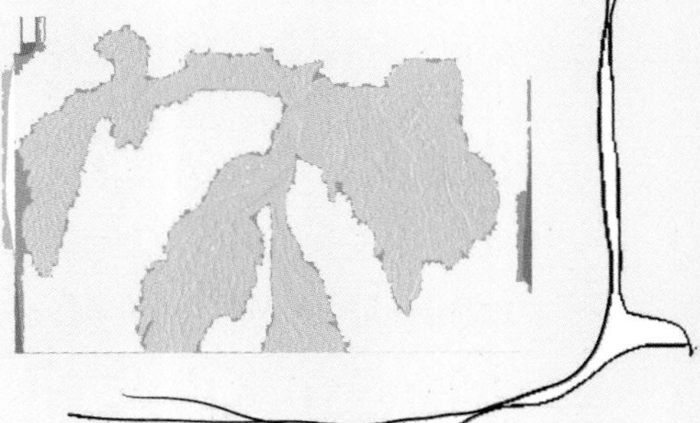

18.1.23

melting snow
five intermittent drips
splashing at the station
well how was I to know
there was a party going on?

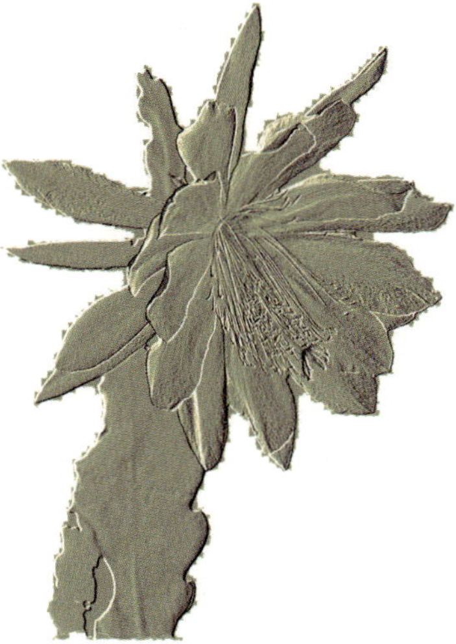

29.1.23

Free Palestine
painted in green
on a wall in Walsall
no weeping no wailing
and no tears

26.1.23 in from the fog
the prima ballerina
wears a scarf
the second coat goes on
like Sunday morning

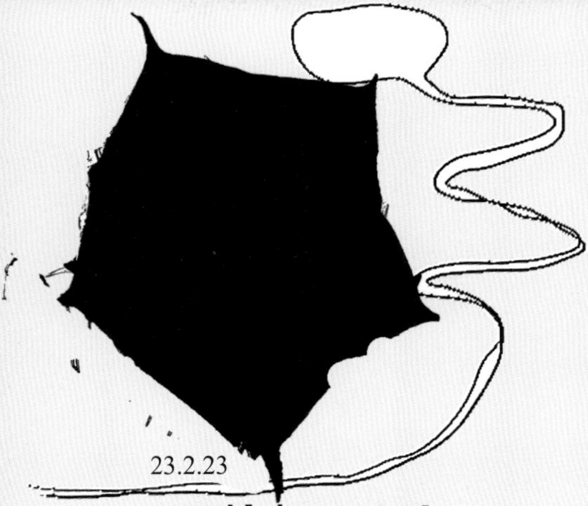

23.2.23

striking out
into the deep blue
one stroke after another
my therapy becomes
my full time job

2.2.23

evil oil games
cooked choked
and taken to the cleaners
no time to sleep
we don't do duvets

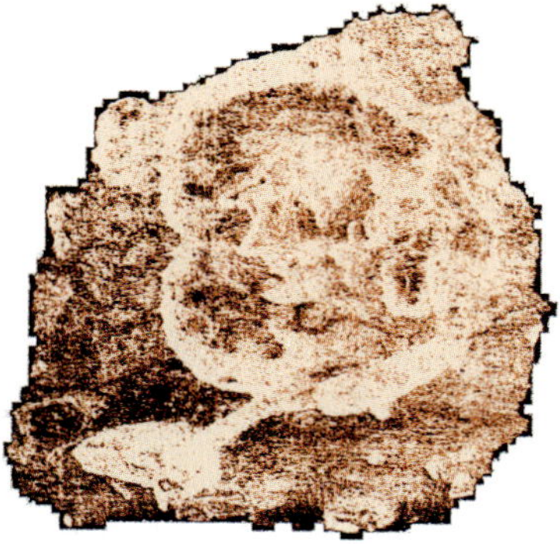

3.3.23

could you summarise
what the poem
was about please?
I start stirring the porridge
a little faster

26.2.23

daschunds and snakes
all kinds of everything
reminds me of you
she whispers in my ear
I can sing a rainbow

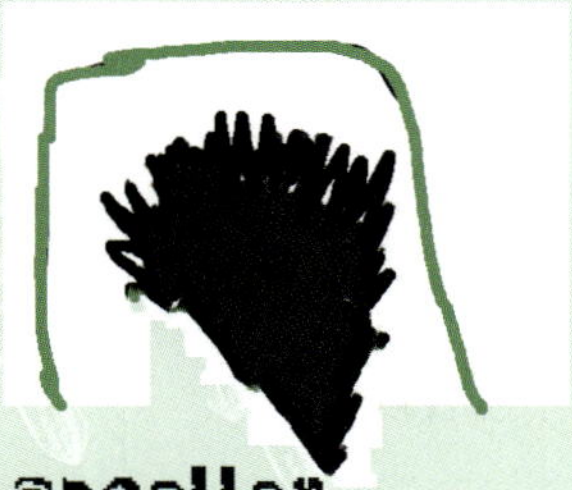

16.3.23

the Shadow Chancellor
plants a money tree
quite partial
to a chocolate Hobnob
the world's tallest jockey

16.3.23 true Zen
a Patrick Star Fish gif
soaks up my stress
crab claws and limpets
in a plastic bucket

2.4.23

fritillaria frenzy
down by the canal
in John's Garden
a mottled bruise
across her left cheek

17.3.23

nothing in this world
that can't be shared
plum blossom
the dull ache in my boots
dissipates

8.4.23

instructional text

poem schema

nocturne in black and gold

confused by street lights

a bird sings into the night

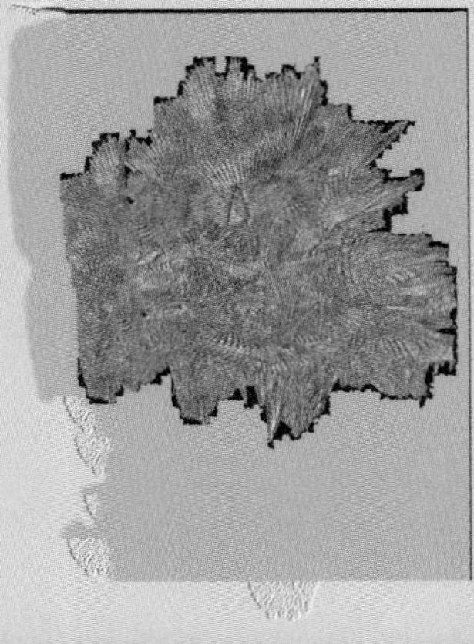

18.4.23

afternoon heat
a three hour pause
in hostilities
Ahmed and Hemetti
sign the constitution

10.4.23

evening chill
unseen fans
sing football songs
to relax her hair
or find her true self

20.4.23

Paul sits and does nothing
Gavin sits with him
the music in their heads
almost three whole days
searching for transformation

24.4.23

in my end
is my beginning
a simple gravestone
small birds flitting
branch to branch

3.5.23 always shower
before entering the pool
the smell of chlorine
awakening somewhere
unexpected

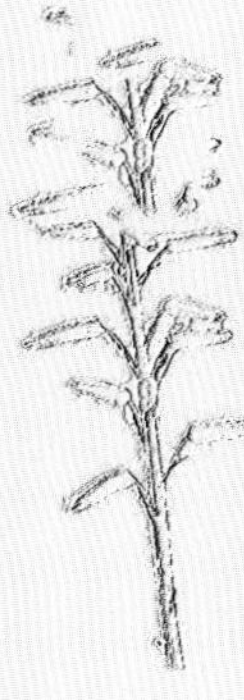

29.4.23

queuing up
for the full english
her heel in his face
dirt and glitter
stuck in the grate

4.5.23

they dress up
for each other
tulips in a pot
serving the Taoiseach
high on Ketamine

4.5.23 effing and blinding
at the TV
swearing his allegiance
a warning letter
served by the police

15.5.23

77 trees
Hilde calls from
the forest in Drenthe
a bug carving itself
into an old pine

4.5.23

the seagulls
and the red devils
throwing the bones
a constellation
of daisies

18.5.23

the daily release
of missiles in various
parts of the world
a giant puffball
under an old oak

18.5.23

all night exploring
the lindwurm in my head
blackbird then robin
a neck support for
sleeping through lectures

17.5.23

not to touch
any tree that might fall
but to let it lie for nine days
polecats, pine martens
and badgers

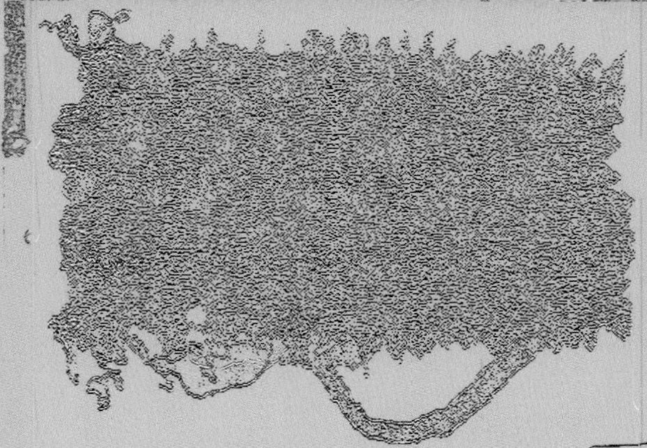

19.5.23 a hen harrier
on the grouse moor
spring trap
ten precious lives
in Tops Friendly Market

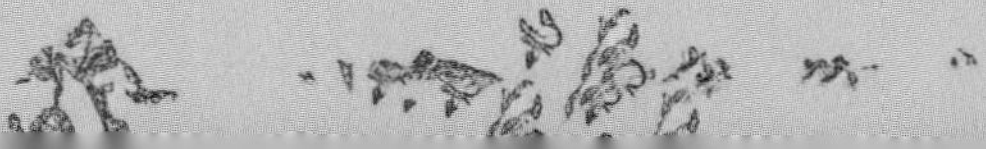

21.5.23

a week off
on the hottest
days of May
relaxing back down
the greasy pole

21.5.23

a song of triumph
and thanksgiving
heavy yellow flowers
that inward eye of yours
she says is overrated

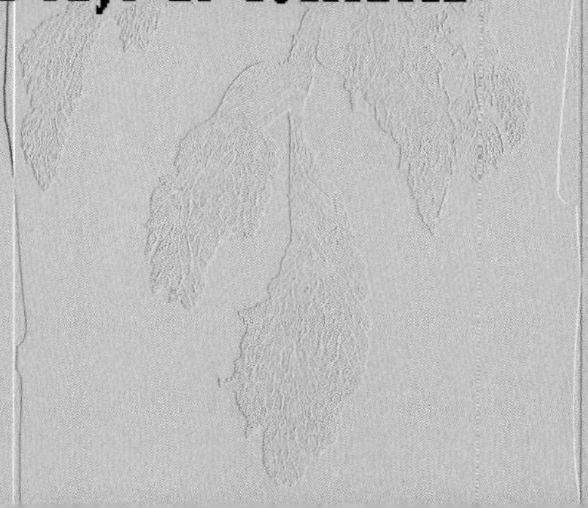

21.5.23

these instructions
are to be retained
by the user
the kids just love
those Swedish meatballs

21.5.23

hanging five
across the forest floor
unfurling ferns
Alice deals one card
face down to each player

27.5.23

to glisten
seven hours into
a peyote high
crisscrossing snail trails
caught in the moonlight

22.5.23

planting a tree
dad leans on his shovel
for a quick smoke
the router blade follows
a winding path

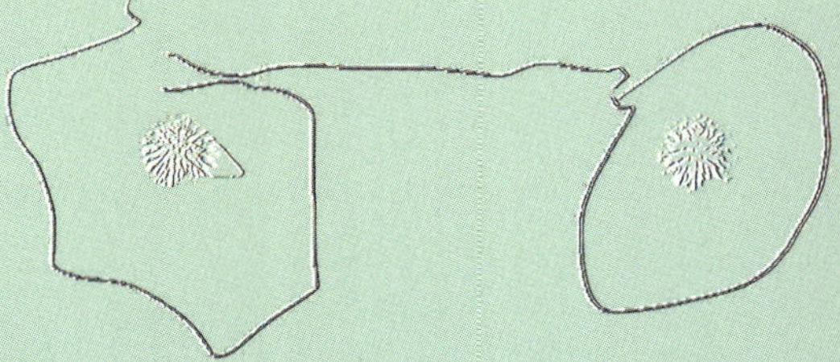

23.5.23

going through customs
the guard checks my pockets
for concealed poems
we kiss three times
on alternating cheeks

23.5.23 midnight rumours
rioters start moving
down Highmead Road
a mother kept waiting
to see her dead son

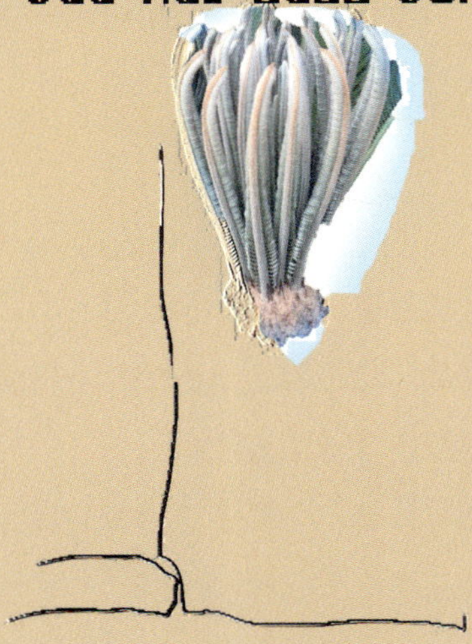

23.5.23

tip some salt into
the water and mix it in
with your forefinger
touching your thumb
teaching without words

23.5.23 (after Bashō)

logged tree
the larger cut end
a harvest moon
a curve of sunburn
fading across his chest

23.5.23

after the kill
she calls for her cubs
leaf litter
Bashō and Beuys
chew the fat

24.5.23

Nan says
it's never too late to lift up
your skirt and dance
counting copper coins
out of an old bottle

24.5.23

things other than plants
the letter zetter reckons
he can make ai moons
the Sea of Tranquility
throws up a splash

24.5.23 still spinning
on that dizzy edge
the moon in my pocket
searching for the origins
of good verses evil

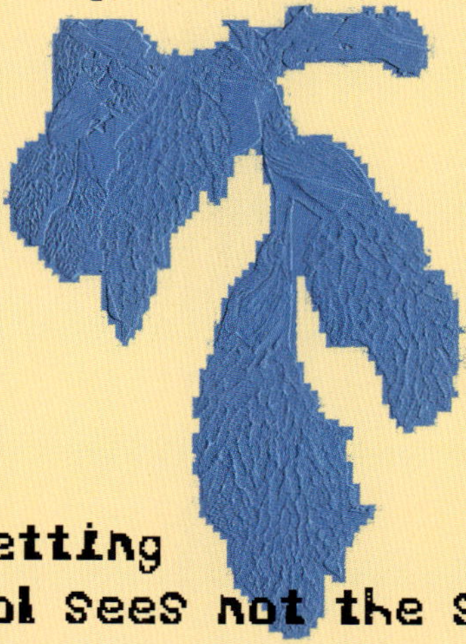

24.5.23

offsetting
a fool sees not the same tree
that a wise man sees
the registration
of colour and time

25.5.23

sister firefly
rereading verses
of the great women poets
a masterpiece drawn
on the back of a wall mirror

25.5.23

flying to Holland
with tangled nets
fishes that will not be caught
sent home from school
with a plastic nit comb

27.5.23

the wolf moon
a body found on the road
to Hoogersmilde
you and your silver bullets
give loving a bad name

27.5.23

attempting to capture
the bass booms
of the bittern
a sound system
with one turntable

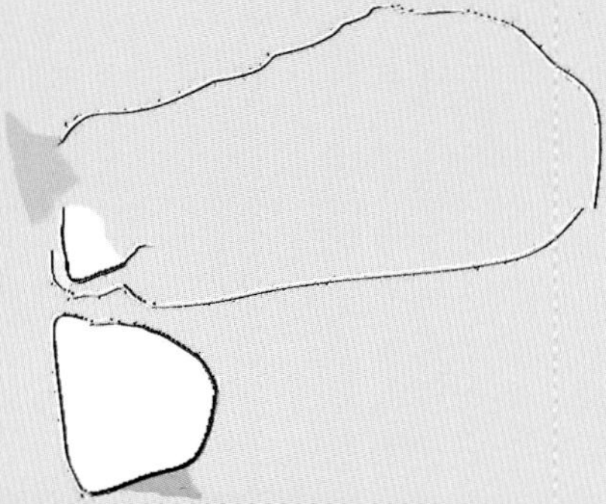

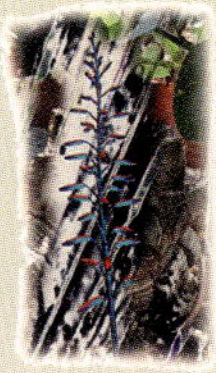

is this the way the universe works?

2023 to 2017

This is a performative book containing #tantwenga verses to be read out loud. Try reading each poem out loud twice and listen for the rhythms and cuts. Hear them and connect with the world, the artists that wrote them. Their lives and those of others. The past and the present. The future too.

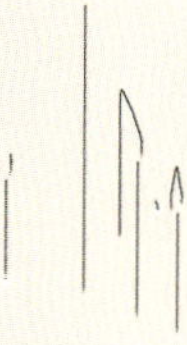

A #tantwenga poem looks like a tanka, a five line Japanese poetry form but it isn't. It's a conversation between a three line haiku-like poem and a two line poem in response – both parts written by either Gavin or Paul, one way or the other. They are connected by the process of link and shift. The two lines linking to the three whilst at the same time shifting away from them.

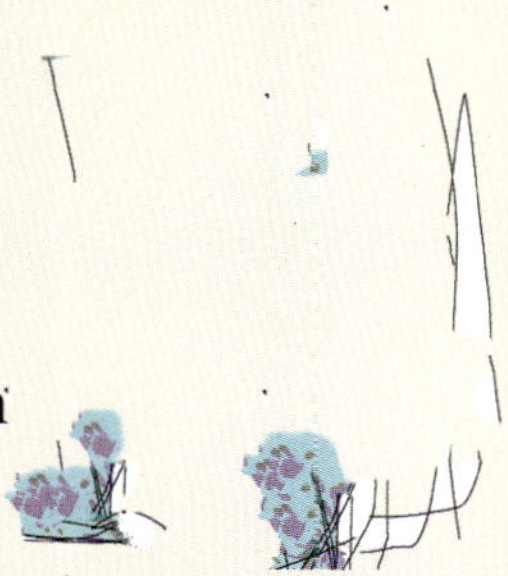

This is a collection of such conversations, written in and out of Twitter, and relating to global issues, overheard conversations, art, poetry and inner thoughts from 2017 to 2023.

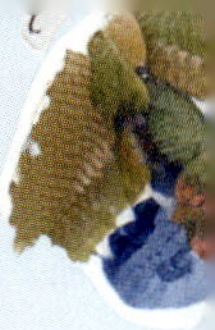

Is this the way the universe works? (555 Verses)

Gavin Wade and Paul Conneally

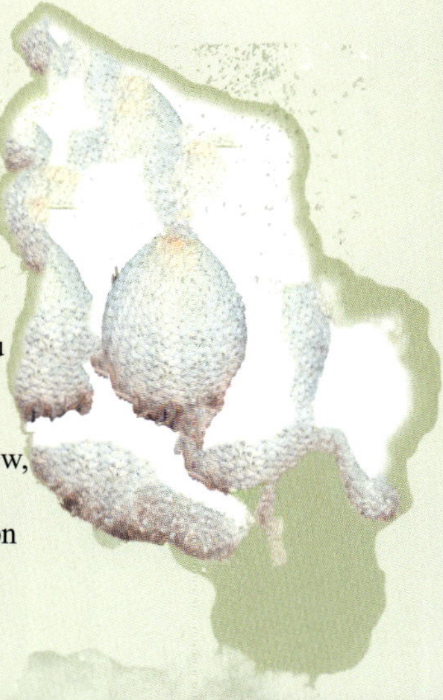

This way around, you can read *555 Verses*. In the centre of the volume is an interview, *You, Me, and Bashō*, and further information about the authors.

To read *77 Verses*, turn the book around.

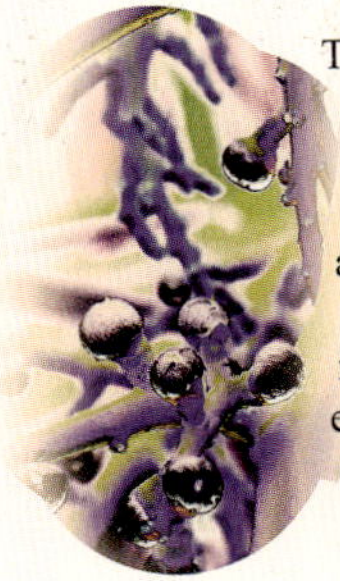

The images accompanying *555 Verses* depict plants from Triangle Garden, Birmingham. The plants are outstanding examples of adaptation strategies in response to changes in environmental conditions, including many cacti, succulents and bananas.

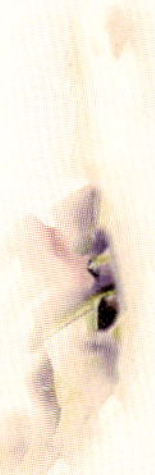

is this the way the universe works?

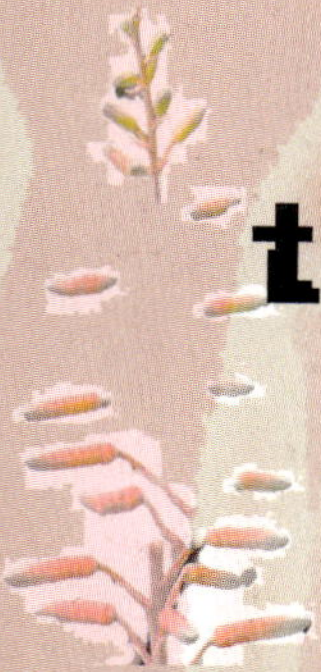

555 verses

Gavin Wade

Paul Conneally